CONSIDER Jesus

A 31-DAY ADVENT DEVOTIONAL

CONSIDER Jesus

MEDITATIONS ON THE PERSON AND WORK OF CHRIST

Nancy DeMoss Wolgemuth

MOODY PUBLISHERS
CHICAGO

Moody Publishers Edition 2026

Content in this book has been compiled and edited from the writing and teaching of Nancy DeMoss Wolgemuth by Lawrence Kimbrough.

Published in association with the literary agency of Wolgemuth & Wilson.

Edited by Anne Christian Buchanan
Cover design: Faceout Studio
Interior Design: Design by Julia, Puckett Smartt
Cover graphic of branches copyright © 2026 by Shutterstock (1984312841). Cover graphic of handdrawn dots copyright © 2026 by Angelina Bambina/Shutterstock (2165017725).
All rights reserved.
Author photo: Nathan Bollinger

ISBN: 978-0-8024-2821-9

Originally delivered by fleets of horse-drawn wagons, the affordable paperbacks from D. L. Moody's publishing house resourced the church and served everyday people. Now, after more than 125 years of publishing and ministry, Moody Publishers' mission remains the same—even if our delivery systems have changed a bit. For more information on other books (and resources) created from a biblical perspective, go to www.moodypublishers.com or write to:

Moody Publishers
820 N. LaSalle Boulevard
Chicago, IL 60610

1 3 5 7 9 10 8 6 4 2

Printed in China

To the Revive Our Hearts *Ministry Partners*
through whose generosity
women around the world are being helped
to see and savor Jesus

CONTENTS

INTRODUCTION

Therefore, holy brothers, you who share in
a heavenly calling, consider Jesus, the apostle
and high priest of our confession,
who was faithful to him who appointed him.

{ HEBREWS 3:1–2 }

MORE THAN ONCE, the writer of the New Testament book of Hebrews urges his readers to "consider" Jesus.

Pause and think of Him. Ponder and focus upon Him. Praise and contemplate Him—this One who is to be "counted worthy" of all glory, much as "the builder of a house has more honor than the house itself" (Heb. 3:3).

How fitting that we would come across this exhortation at a time of year when the "house" is being prepared for Him. The lights, the tree, the candles and candy tins, even the dishes and the hand towels—they all say *Christmas*. In cities, towns, and villages throughout much of the world, the occasion of Jesus' coming has created an environment where people delight in brightening their homes to varying degrees of glory.

Yet no matter how impressive the decorating skills—and no matter how high the level of expectation we place upon this special, sparkly window of time each year—the real glory properly belongs only to the Builder of the "house" of Christmas.

To Jesus.

Consider Jesus—the Architect and Designer of the season.

In one sense, the choice to concentrate a collection of Advent devotional readings on Jesus sounds altogether natural and obvious. What—or Who—else would we focus on?

Well, the truth is, our Christmas house can be filled with many things besides Christ, even beneath the banner of celebrating Him. That's why if we're not deliberate in giving *Him* our time and attention, our awareness of His presence can easily become artificial, even inconsequential.

So with the Advent season before us, I invite you into a month of daily reflections in which the sole purpose is to keep our eyes on Jesus. In the process, we will deepen our relationship with Him, and our hearts will be freshly stirred as we consider what makes God's gift of His Son—the baby Jesus—the perfect and only plan for our redemption.

But that's not all we'll be doing . . . and here's why.

Some years, December draws to a close, and all we've done is marvel again at the story of the Christ child in the manger—which we should! The love and mercy, the wisdom and wonder of God on display in Bethlehem ought never fail to move us to worship. Maybe we'll have even stopped to ponder what the manger has to do with the cross and the empty tomb—and we should do that too. But shouldn't we also keep looking beyond what we know of Jesus' earthly life to what Scripture says He is doing *now*—today?

For though Christmas often rushes past us as if slipping through our fingers, it actually catches us each year in the middle of eternity—where Jesus *is*. Where He continues to love and bless us, to change and transform us. Where His birth and death and life and reality never stop directly impacting us each day we live.

My desire in this season is to fill my home not only with Christmas, but with the very present reality of the Lord Jesus Christ. I hope you'll be doing the same. And as we turn the page on this last month of the year, I pray your heart will be filled with wonder and gratitude.

Join me now in wanting more than just a place to house another holiday season.

Come along as together we *consider Jesus*.

Nancy

PS: As you move through this book, you'll notice I've included some additional elements to accompany each day's main devotional reading. But please remember that the goal isn't to complete all the pieces; it's to experience everything

God desires this season to be for you. As you make room in your heart to consider Him during these days, be prepared for Him to fill every space with Himself.

DECEMBER 1

FOR YOUR CONSIDERATION

Consider him who endured from sinners
such hostility against himself,
so that you may not grow weary or fainthearted.

{ HEBREWS 12:3 }

CHRISTMAS IS NOT JUST A HOLIDAY like other holidays. It's not a spring Sunday set aside to honor one of our parents. It's not a summer celebration of national pride and patriotism. It's not even a fall gathering of family and friends with ample servings of thanksgiving on the menu—though I really do love that holiday, and I hope yours was truly special and worshipful this year.

Christmas, though, is different. Christmas is meant to remind us that Christianity, while technically classified as one of the world's major religions, is not at heart a religion at all. It is a *relationship* that focuses on a *Person*. It is not just a means of practicing our faith. It is Christ in me. It is Christ in you. That is Christianity.

And that is Christmas.

It is Jesus—the center, the core, the essence of our lives. And we must not allow the "holiday" to distract us from this great truth or cause us to lose our focus on who He is.

I believe that's why you're here. It's why I'm here too. Together we're admitting what the holiday aspect of Christmas is capable of doing to us.

We get busy.

Our lists overtake us.

Our memories, whether good or bad or a casserole mixture of the two, create an undertow that can easily engulf us in Christmas culture rather than helping us consider Jesus.

So hear that word again today. "Consider him."

Interestingly, the "consider him" of Hebrews 12 is a slightly different original word than the "consider Jesus" of Hebrews 3:1. That earlier mention is an encouragement to stop, as in a moment of temptation, and think of Him. "For because he himself has suffered when tempted, he is able to help those who are being tempted" (Heb. 2:18). Hebrews 3:1 urges us to think about that fact when we are tempted.

But the "consider him" in Hebrews 12:3 comes in the context of running the "race that is set before us" (12:1). It is an appeal to think *repeatedly* of Him—over and over again—as we move forward in our lives, knowing we'll never have the endurance to finish the "race" if we let our attention drift elsewhere.

Our only hope for making it through Christmas and (more importantly) through life is to look to Jesus, "the founder and perfecter of our faith, who for the joy that was set before him endured the cross, despising the shame, and is seated at the right hand of the throne of God" (v. 2). To look and look and keep on looking. To never look anywhere else.

Perhaps already, this far out from Christmas Day, you can feel yourself growing a bit "weary or fainthearted" from the demands you've come to expect this time of year.

If that is true for you, let me give you something to consider today and each day of this season—again and again, over and over.

Consider Jesus.

{Prayer}

Lord, fully capture my attention this Christmas. Help me savor You and stay enthralled with You above every activity and event and highlight of this season. Thank You for bringing Your presence so close. May I never tire of looking for You and longing for You—repeatedly, unceasingly. Today and forever.

{ *Keep Reading* }

1 SAMUEL 12:20–24

"Consider what great things he has done for you." (v. 24)

PSALM 143:5–10

"I meditate on all that you have done." (v. 5)

1 PETER 4:7–11

"That in everything God may be glorified through Jesus Christ." (v. 11)

{ *Consider* }

What are the things that tend to draw your focus away from Jesus during the Christmas season? How could you adjust your plans or expectations to keep Him truly central?

Jesus

HIS SAVING PURPOSE

But when the fullness of time had come,
God sent forth his Son, born of woman,
born under the law, to redeem those
who were under the law,
so that we might receive adoption as sons.

{ GALATIANS 4:4–5 }

DECEMBER 2

GIVER OF BLESSING

So God created man in his own image,
in the image of God he created him;
male and female he created them.
And God blessed them.

{ GENESIS 1:27–28 }

"MERRY CHRISTMAS!" Don't those words feel like a blessing—a Christmas blessing we receive and also share with others?

Actually, if you'll notice, we share words of blessing with one another all year long. Implied blessing is tucked inside every "Good morning" and "Good night," inside every "How are you doing?" and "Have a nice day." Each is an expression of hope for another person's happiness and welfare.

"But those are just habits," you might say. "They're just social conventions." And that's true to a point. But *why* do such expressions come automatically to people's lips, even if they're spoken without much thought? Why feel any need for speaking them at all, even to total strangers? Why do we learn those habits and follow those social conventions wherever we go—from the office elevator to the grocery-store counter to the drive-through window?

It's because God created each one of us to bless and be blessed.

And He created us with hearts that long most of all for His blessing.

We were purposely made with an emptiness inside us for God to continually fill. We depend on Him for our existence, for our every thought and action. And from the opening pages of His story, we see Him doing it. We see Him blessing.

God's very first words to the first man and woman were words of blessing: "God blessed them." He blessed them with relationship and opportunity, with a future of growth and multiplication. He blessed them with purpose and responsibility and provision. All quarters of His creation, from the moment He placed humankind within them, were pictures of His favor, His abundance, His fruitfulness.

His blessing.

All blessing began with God. And all blessing ultimately comes from Him. Life itself, including the most routine, familiar days, remains an ever-opening gift of divine favor. We are constantly receiving blessing from our original Blesser. We've been made this way, made by God, not only to long for blessing but to be blessed by Him.

And that's how we arrive at this blessed moment of year. Christmas—the Christ—is God's ultimate Blessing, given from the heart of One who's been blessing us, who's been blessing you, from the beginning of time.

As you begin turning your thoughts more consistently now to your celebration of Christmas, begin by recognizing the great blessing of the birth of Christ. "The blessing of the LORD makes rich," the Bible says (Prov. 10:22)—rich with eternal reminders of how Jesus' appearance in the flesh has changed our lives, rich with opportunities both for receiving this message ourselves and for sharing it with others.

"Merry Christmas," we say. "Merry Christmas," we hear.

But each time you say it and each time you receive it, be reminded of the source of all true joy and blessing—God Himself . . . loving and blessing His people through Jesus, come down from heaven to earth.

{ *Prayer* }

Lord, I praise You today for things which
I cannot fully fathom, yet which compel me even
at the fringes of my understanding to fall before
You in worship. Thank You for the incalculable
blessing You have given me in Jesus.
I receive Him with humble joy. May I share Him
with extravagant generosity.

{ Keep Reading }

DEUTERONOMY 28:1–6

"All these blessings shall come upon you and overtake you." (v. 2)

PSALM 65:9–13

"You visit the earth and water it;
you greatly enrich it." (v. 9)

JAMES 1:16–18

"Every good gift and every perfect gift is from above." (v. 17)

{ Consider }

How might this awareness of others' deep need for His blessing affect even your Christmas greetings this year? How could your "Merry Christmas" help fill others with His joy?

DECEMBER 3

THE CURSE AND THE CURE

Christ redeemed us from the curse of the law
by becoming a curse for us—for it is written,
"Cursed is everyone who is hanged on a tree."

{ GALATIANS 3:13 }

NO SOONER DOES THE BIBLE BEGIN, with its lush accounts of creation and beauty and the surge of new life, than it descends into tragedy. I never fail to feel jolted by Genesis 3—the fall of Adam and Eve into open rebellion. It's as if someone opens a can of dark paint and slings the full, contaminating contents over a beautiful canvas. The picture is instantly wrecked. The whole big, beautiful world becomes cold and darkened.

Cursed.

There's no sugarcoating it—this curse, which even now casts its long shadow across the earth as a result of that devastating episode. We hear some of it in God's words to the first couple after their fall into sin—words of pain and sweat and dust and death (Gen. 3:16–19).

Let us never sweeten our picture of God to the extent that we fail to see Him capable of imposing a curse on sin. His justice demands it. In His holiness He cannot do otherwise. Our disobedience is not a slight to Him; it is a grave and punishable offense. Sin must always be punished.

But the fact that God came to those first humans even after their sin and betrayal, that He chose to step again into that ravaged Eden—never miss the stunning mercy of that moment. "They heard the sound of the LORD God walking in the garden in the cool of the day" (Gen. 3:8). He had come to deliver an announcement of cursing, yes. But at least He had *come*.

God came. And His coming in that moment tells us something beautiful this Christmas.

The rest of the Old Testament is a gritty, glorious portrait of God's coming to His people again and again and again, reminding them of how their sin had doomed them to His curse, but how it could never diminish His original desire to bless. Humankind had taken a picture-perfect setting and made it uninhabitable, but God came into that cursed place and declared that He would rectify this situation.

That's why Jesus came.

He walked into a world that was broken and wrecked. Everything the curse entails—hardship, struggle, pain, grief, heartache, turmoil, limitation, condemnation—Jesus came to encounter. Long before God came into the garden pronouncing

His curse, He had already planned for Someone to come and stand in our place, to take the full brunt of that curse for us, to bear the righteous punishment our sin deserves.

The curse was no small thing. The cross could be no small thing either.

We can never really experience God's blessing—or the blessing of Christmas—if we've not felt what it means to be under His curse. If sin grieved the heart of God enough to cost the death of His only Son, the cure He delivered should cause our hearts to respond with an acceptable sacrifice of our own . . . the sacrifice of praise.

{ *Prayer* }

Father, may I never minimize the weight of my sin,
seeing it as insignificant or merely regrettable,
something I should be able to work around.
You knew from the beginning that there could be
no work-around, that the only fix for the curse
was sending Jesus right into the center of it.
Praise You, Lord, for refusing to stop at my failure.
Thank You for showing me the great mercy of
Your blessing.

{ Keep Reading }

DEUTERONOMY 30:15–20

"I have set before you life and death, blessing and curse." (v. 19)

PSALM 109:26–31

"Let them curse, but you will bless!" (v. 28)

REVELATION 22:1–5

"No longer will there be anything accursed." (v. 3)

{ Consider }

How have you experienced the gravity of sin's curse in your life? How do you still feel its consequences in and around you? Remember, "He comes to make His blessings flow far as the curse is found."[1]

DECEMBER 4

FLAWLESS PERFORMANCE

He is the mediator of a new covenant,
so that those who are called may receive
the promised eternal inheritance.

{ HEBREWS 9:15 }

NEARING HIS DEATH, Moses instructed the children of Israel to conduct a little ceremony (Deut. 27) when they entered the Promised Land. They were to divide into two equal groups and position themselves in front of two mountains—Mount Ebal and Mount Gerizim—that stood opposite each other in Canaan. The two groups would thus be facing each other. The Levites (priests) were to stand between the assembled congregation and read aloud the words of the law. And the people on either side were to hear and respond with a collective, "Amen!"

Picture this scene, which eventually took place at the end of Joshua 8. The priests loudly proclaimed together a single line from the law of God, and the Israelites—in stunning antiphonal effect—roared their united agreement. *Amen! Amen! Amen!* Over and over again. Then, in one final summary statement, the Levites called out, "Cursed be anyone who does not confirm the words of this law by doing them" (Deut. 27:26). And with triumphant resolution, all the people shouted, rejoicing at the echo: *AMEN!*

I'm sure they meant it—just as we meant it last Christmas when we resolved that "next year" we would not let our lives become so busy, chaotic, and uncontrollable that we couldn't settle in and spend the season in worship, in true joy, in simplicity, sharing, and wonder.

But the Israelites, even after that pivotal and unforgettable moment, failed to "confirm the words" of the law. They broke their covenant with God again and again. And we, too, often fail to live up to what we have promised to do. We, too, are covenant breakers. And though we tend to think that we're not so bad, that God will surely negotiate terms with us, bearing in mind the specifics of our situation, that's not what the Bible tells us.

"Let a curse be on the man who does not obey the words of this covenant" (Jer. 11:3 CSB). That's Old Testament.

"Everyone who does not do everything written in the book of the law is cursed" (Gal. 3:10 CSB). That's New Testament.

We're surrounded on both sides, as the Israelites were at Ebal and Gerizim. Saying what we mean, but not always doing what we say.

That's why we must consider Jesus. For while God will never adjust His stance on what breaking the covenant involves, He has promised us this: He will accept a substitute—the One who "offered himself without blemish to God" (Heb. 9:14), who fulfilled through His perfect life every jot and tittle and line item of the law that we, if left to ourselves, have no hope of obeying.

Praise God we do not arrive at this Christmas to "blazing fire and darkness and gloom and a tempest" (Heb. 12:18), to the prospect of utter destruction for our sins. We come instead "to Jesus, the mediator of a new covenant" (v. 24), to the secured promise of eternal relationship with Him because of what God has done through Christ for covenant breakers like us.

{ *Prayer* }

O God, how I thank You for the wonder of Jesus,
that You would send Him to this earth to die for us,
having lived the perfect life You require of us.
I recognize my helplessness today, my total
dependence on Your grace. And I thank You that
because of Jesus, my Covenant Keeper, I can now
truly live in freedom and obedience before You.
To which I wholeheartedly respond: Amen!

{ Keep Reading }

JOSHUA 8:30–35

"He read all the words of the law, the blessing and the curse." (v. 34)

PSALM 5:11–12

"You bless the righteous, O Lord." (v. 12)

HEBREWS 9:11–15

". . . since a death has occurred that redeems them." (v. 15)

{ Consider }

What does it mean to you to be saved from the curse of breaking the law? What are some fitting responses to escaping ultimate punishment?

DECEMBER 5

FOR MY CLEANSING, THIS MY PLEA

When the time came for their purification according to the Law of Moses, they brought him up to Jerusalem.

{ LUKE 2:22 }

IF YOU WERE ASKED TO NAME A LOCATION in Scripture that sounds about as far away from Christmas as possible, Leviticus 12 might be a good candidate. *Leviticus*—strewn with last January's derailed attempts at reading through the Bible in a year.

And yet in one tiny eight-verse chapter of that book—tucked in between detailed definitions of clean versus unclean animals and prescriptions for how to safely handle horrific diseases of the skin—we read words that suddenly transport us to the tender image of Mary and Joseph entering the temple in Jerusalem with their weeks-old baby Jesus.

Luke 2 tells us that the time had come for Mary's "purification"—the conclusion of a forty-day period in which a new mother, having shed copious amounts of blood during the birthing process, was able to be declared ritually clean under the Mosaic law. And Leviticus 12 explains exactly what that ceremony entailed. The law called for the sacrifice of a year-old lamb for a burnt offering. But it made allowance for couples like Mary and Joseph who couldn't afford a lamb, requiring them instead to bring only "two turtledoves or two pigeons" (v. 8), which the priest would then offer for the woman's atonement.

Blood was being spilled everywhere in the temple that day, as it was every day. Fountains of blood streamed down from the altar as a means of restoring the relationship between sinful humans and a holy God. "Under the law almost everything is purified with blood," the writer of Hebrews would later write, "and without the shedding of blood there is no forgiveness of sins" (Heb. 9:22).

So into this scene—in an unmistakable link between Leviticus 12 and Luke 2—Mary came meekly forward, having traversed the six miles from Bethlehem to Jerusalem with her husband and baby. Clutched in one arm, perhaps, she held her compulsory sacrifices, offering a pair of birds to the Lord out of obedience to His Word, to be slain for her purification. But surely clutched in her other arm was the infant Lamb of God, who—also in obedience to His Word, and willingly—would one day offer Himself not only for Mary's sins, but for your sins and my sins and the sins of the world.

It's such a striking picture, made all the more precious

because it reaches back so many centuries into the heaviness of the Old Testament and rushes through first-century Palestine on its way to us here today, this Christmas. It reminds us that the gospel is as old as it is new and that the blood of Jesus still purifies.

> Oh! precious is the flow
> That makes me white as snow; No other fount I know,
> Nothing but the blood of Jesus.[2]

{ *Prayer* }

Father, thank You for giving us this glimpse into what You've done, from before time began, to make atonement for our sin. Thank You for the purity that even now is mine because of the unstained blood of Jesus, which stains me purest white in Your presence. Help me walk with a forgiven conscience through this Christmas season, filled by the old story, filled with new praise.

{ Keep Reading }

PSALM 18:25–28

"With the purified you show yourself pure." (v. 26)

MALACHI 3:3–4

"He will sit as a refiner and purifier of silver." (v. 3)

1 PETER 1:22–23

"Love one another earnestly from a pure heart." (v. 22)

{ Consider }

The gospel enables us to walk in "love that issues from a pure heart and a good conscience and a sincere faith" (1 Tim. 1:5). What might be keeping you from experiencing these freedoms today?

Jesus

HIS ETERNAL DEITY

For in him the whole fullness of deity dwells bodily,
and you have been filled in him,
who is the head of all rule and authority.

{ COLOSSIANS 2:9–10 }

DECEMBER 6

HE IS JESUS; HE IS GOD

In him the whole fullness of deity dwells bodily.

{ COLOSSIANS 2:9 }

THE WORLD DOESN'T MIND THAT THERE'S A JESUS. If for no other reason, they sure do love Christmas!

And though it may come as a surprise to some believers, who've perhaps grown accustomed to an "us versus them" mentality, people outside the church are generally okay with Jesus. Not only is He well-known in general culture; He is also largely admired.

A Google search today on the single word *Jesus* returned approximately 1.4 *billion* results (in just "0.39 seconds"). And while it would be impossible to look up all the flagged posts, articles, and other internet references, I'm sure that a good number come from people who don't consider themselves Christians, but who concede that Jesus is still worth studying and learning about.

What they *don't* accept, however, is that Jesus is God—

because if that's true, He is no longer simply a historical figure who went around doing good and saying a lot of wise, kind things. If Jesus is God, He stops being merely a great moral teacher and becomes Someone who has all authority and power, Someone before whom all humanity stands accountable.

And the world does majorly mind *that* part.

It's what rankled the self-righteous class of Jesus' day, who often admitted, "Teacher, you have spoken well" (Luke 20:39). Jesus' ability to see through a situation and make penetrating observations about life and the law impressed them. But when it came to His saying things like, "From now on you will see the Son of Man seated at the right hand of Power and coming on the clouds of heaven" (Matt. 26:64), that's when they flew into a rage. That's when they knew He must die. "Blasphemy," they shouted (v. 65). In claiming to be God, Jesus had gone too far.

Since then, throughout history, we see this ongoing counterassault against Jesus' claim to deity. Many modern-day religions, in fact, though perhaps sincere and devout in their worship of God, relegate Jesus to second-rung status—as *a* Son of God, but not *the* Son of God, as an angel or prophet or perfect man, but not on par with God Himself. People by and large remain intrigued by Him, fascinated by Him, and willing to give Him a place on history's list of inspiring figures, as long as He stays somewhat understandable and therefore, ultimately, under their control.

But Jesus *is* God . . . unapologetically God. The wonder of Christmas is that "God was manifested in the flesh" (1 Tim. 3:16 NKJV). If not, the whole structure of Christianity crumbles. But if so—and it is most assuredly so—our celebration of Christmas can be not only a winter excuse for expressions of human love and kindness, but an opportunity to receive again the love of God for us.

{ *Prayer* }

Holy God, I come to You today in Jesus' name, recognizing Him for who He is. Lord Jesus, I worship You. You are my God, and I will praise You. You are my God, and I bow my knee to You. And because of Your atoning grace for me and the gift of repentance and faith you have given me, I will spend eternity around Your throne, worshiping You and You alone.

{ *Keep Reading* }

PSALM 118:26–29

“You are my God, and I will give thanks to you.” (v. 28)

ISAIAH 25:6–9

“Behold, this is our God; we have waited for him.” (v. 9)

LUKE 7:18–23

“Blessed is the one who is not offended by me.” (v. 23)

{ *Consider* }

What are the consequences of demoting Jesus from His rightful place of deity?

What difference does it make to this world and in your life that Jesus is who He claimed to be?

DECEMBER 7

ETERNALLY YOURS

"Father, glorify me in your own presence with the glory that I had with you before the world existed."

{ JOHN 17:5 }

EVER SINCE I WAS A LITTLE GIRL, I've been a huge fan of biographies. I've read perhaps hundreds of them through the years. And I've noticed that the early chapters of a biography almost always include details about the subject's birth and about the particular era when that person entered the world.

I've only encountered one biography, however, of a person who lived before he or she was in the womb!

We lightheartedly comment sometimes that little boys and girls come from heaven. But they don't really come from heaven. God creates them. He chooses the time and place for their conception and birth. They don't live anywhere else before that.

Jesus, however . . . has always been.

Jesus *is*. "Before Abraham was, I am," He told His disciples (John 8:58).

This is an enormous, vitally important teaching of Scripture, and numerous biblical examples bear witness to the truth of it. Today though, I'll mention only one.

Do you remember the jaw-dropping scene in Isaiah 6 that begins, "In the year that King Uzziah died I saw the Lord sitting upon a throne, high and lifted up; and the train of his robe filled the temple" (v. 1)? The call of angels' voices and the smell of smoke and the quaking of the ground underneath his feet reduced the prophet to a puddle of repentance. He had seen the Lord! And even we ourselves, looking on by proxy, can never forget it.

The Gospels contain more than two dozen direct quotations from the book of Isaiah, far more than any other prophetic writing, presented as proof to New Testament readers that Jesus is the direct fulfillment of God's plan from ages past. Interesting. Why would Isaiah lead the way in this department? John's answer: "Isaiah said these things because he saw his glory and spoke of him" (John 12:41). In other words, the "high and lifted up" Lord that Isaiah saw hundreds of years before Jesus was born was the glory of Christ Himself, one with the Father.

And Jesus had been that way forever. Just as He has no end, He had no beginning. "In the beginning was the Word [Jesus], and the Word was with God, and the Word was God" (John 1:1). Before anything else existed, the Son was already experiencing close, intimate communion and fellowship with the Father—distinct from the Father, yet one with the Father.

And then came . . . Christmas. The preexistent Christ became the child in the manger. He left behind the joy of perfect fellowship with the Father to come down to our prodigal planet, so that we might one day experience through Him the oneness with the Father that He had enjoyed forever.

> Out of the ivory palaces,
> Into a world of woe,
> Only his great, eternal love
> Made my Savior go.[3]

{ *Prayer* }

I worship You, Lord, the eternally preexistent God. Thank You that even though You were perfectly complete in the Trinity—loving and being loved—You loved us enough that You would come here to be hated and murdered. I experience oneness with the Father today only because You have made it possible. Help me always stay close to You, Lord Jesus.

{ Keep Reading }

PSALM 138:7–8

"Your steadfast love, O Lord, endures forever." (v. 8)

ISAIAH 48:12–16

"From the time it came to be I have been there." (v. 16)

COLOSSIANS 1:15–17

"He is before all things, and in him all things
hold together." (v. 17)

{ Consider }

What do the eternal existence of Jesus
and His oneness with the Father mean
for our relationship with God?

DECEMBER 8

A JOY FOREVER

I was beside him, like a master workman,
and I was daily his delight,
rejoicing before him always.

{ PROVERBS 8:30 }

PROVERBS 8 APPEARS IN SCRIPTURE as a personification of wisdom, in which this age-old virtue assumes a voice and describes its own origins and properties. But many commentators believe this colorful slice of biblical literature actually refers to Christ, the "wisdom of God" (1 Cor. 1:24).

It's not hard to see it . . . as when "wisdom" speaks of being present with the Lord at creation, of already being in existence

> when he made firm the skies above,
> when he established the fountains of the deep,
> when he assigned to the sea its limit. (Proverbs 8:28–29)

We know from other passages that Jesus was present with the Father at Creation, not as a spectator or bystander, but as an active participant in the framing of the world. He was there devising the plan for our salvation, working together with the other members of the Trinity, from eternity past.

But notice, too, His demeanor. Take note of the tenor of His heart, as Proverbs 8 describes it:

> I was daily his delight,
> rejoicing before him always,
> rejoicing in his inhabited world
> and delighting in the children of man. (vv. 30–31)

Delight. Enjoyment. Pleasure.

Rejoicing. Play, laughter, making merry.

Throughout all time, in other words, Jesus was celebrating with His Father, delighting in what they were doing, rejoicing as they made plans for us and observed the inhabited world.

I love this biblical affirmation that we serve a happy God, a joyful Savior. We can say it without risk of sounding trite or disrespectful because Scripture itself reveals this to be true. The Persons of the Trinity enjoy being together. They find pleasure in each other's company. When we think about why we're (usually) eager to gather with family and friends at Christmas—to laugh, to share, to happily interact—well, it's because such interaction is the nature of the One who made us.

So it's hardly a wonder to hear Jesus say, in opening His heart to the disciples, "These things I have spoken to you so that My joy may be in you, and that your joy may be made full" (John 15:11 NASB).

Or "Until now you have asked nothing in my name. Ask, and you will receive, that your joy may be full" (John 16:24).

Or in prayer to His Father: "Now I am coming to you, and these things I speak in the world, that they may have my joy fulfilled in themselves" (John 17:13).

We were made to experience joy. God *wants* us to experience joy. He desires that we live with the vibrancy of this fruit of the Spirit inside us, coursing naturally from the Vine where purest love and enjoyment have been pulsing forever.

So, joy to the world? Yes, indeed . . . because there was joy, eternal joy, before the world ever came to be.

{ *Prayer* }

Lord, thank You that in the midst of a life that can sometimes be so hard, You not only make joy available to me but also desire it for me. I confess that I too easily see sternness and coldness in You, assuming I will never meet with Your approval. Help me rejoice today in Your grace and remember that You find joy in what You've done and are doing with me.

{ Keep Reading }

PSALM 89:14–18

"Happy are the people who know the joyful shout." (v. 15 CSB)

ISAIAH 62:3–5

"So shall your God rejoice over you." (v. 5)

1 JOHN 1:1–4

"We are writing these things so that our joy may be complete." (v. 4)

{ Consider }

Joy doesn't often come naturally to us, but perhaps it would if we more eagerly sought for it. How might you keep yourself reminded in this season that Jesus is rejoicing over you and that His joy is the legacy He has given you through His work and ministry on your behalf?

DECEMBER 9

PRIOR ANNOUNCEMENT

"She will bear a son,
and you shall call his name Jesus,
for he will save his people from their sins."

{ MATTHEW 1:21 }

WE'RE GETTING TO THAT TIME OF YEAR when we start to see a lot of "top ten" lists recounting the most notable happenings from the year that is quickly drawing to a close. One of the lists that intrigues me is the annual top ten list of baby names that parents selected for their newborns during that year. It's fascinating to see how the current year's choices compare with those from decades ago and how some of the names that were once so commonplace are now almost completely unused.

That list is a cultural statement, obviously. But more personally, it speaks to the exciting process of selecting a name for a child who's coming, narrowing down the field of favorites until the expectant parents land on one with just the right sound or rhythm or meaning or family tie. You may hear them talking about the name or being asked about it all the time, often right up to the moment of their son or daughter's birth.

In Jesus' case, however, the Father had already given Him a name many centuries before His conception. Actually, in the course of Scripture, numerous names were given to this One who would come to earth in the fullness of time:

> For to us a child is born,
> to us a son is given;
> and the government shall be upon his shoulder,
> and his name shall be called
> Wonderful Counselor, Mighty God,
> Everlasting Father, Prince of Peace. (Isaiah 9:6)

This was no ordinary birth: "The Holy Spirit will come upon you, and the power of the Most High will overshadow you; therefore the child to be born will be called holy—the Son of God" (Luke 1:35).

And His is no ordinary name: "To him all the prophets bear witness," the apostle Peter said, "that everyone who believes in him receives forgiveness of sins through his name" (Acts 10:43). Truly, the entirety of the Bible has been written "so that you may believe that Jesus is the Christ, the Son of God, and that by believing you may have life in his name" (John 20:31).

In His name.

In the precious name of *Jesus*. Savior.

As you reflect on His nativity name in this Christmas season, hear in those two recognizable syllables not only the assured sound of your salvation, but also the "deep calls to deep" (Psalm 42:7) purposes of God echoing across time, having been chosen *before* time. Realize that His name was already known and selected not only before He was born, but before *anyone* was born.

Each person's name says a lot.

But only one name—the name of Jesus—says everything.

{ *Prayer* }

Father, what a gift you gave this world when You gave the name *Jesus* to Your only Son. The unveiling of Your eternal plan. The promise of eternal salvation through His life, death, and resurrection. Praise You, Lord, in Jesus' name.

{ Keep Reading }

PSALM 48:9–14

"This is God,
our God forever and ever." (v. 14)

ISAIAH 59:20–21

"A Redeemer will come to Zion." (v. 20)

2 THESSALONIANS 1:11–12

"That the name of our Lord Jesus may be glorified in you." (v. 12)

{ Consider }

Sometimes it's enough to simply meditate on His name: *Jesus*. Let His name flow from your lips with reverence and joy, with hope and worship.

DECEMBER 10

SINCE JESUS IS GOD

No one has ever seen God; God the only Son,
who is at the Father's side, he has made him known.

{ JOHN 1:18 }

THE LANGUAGE OF EACH GENERATION coalesces around certain words that define its underlying worldview. Certainly, one of the words that dominates today's thinking is *tolerance*, often expressed as resistance to its archvillain *intolerance*.

Intolerance, then, has become a dirty word in our age, one from which we're supposed to feel pressure to recoil, so as not to be associated with its hardened stances. But if something is true, a person's belief in that thing is not intolerant—whether it be the wisdom of monthly budgeting or the body's need for sleep or the sanctity of one's marriage.

Intolerance in such cases means to defend, protect, and honor a truth that results in good to those who live by it. So count me as one who is "intolerant" in terms of what Jesus' deity means.

Why is this truth—that Jesus is God—so important to

defend, even at the risk of being thought intolerant? Consider its implications for our faith and life:

First, *Jesus' deity is what makes it possible for us to know God.*

How often have you seen in someone's face a clear resemblance to one of his or her parents? That's what the Son of God gives us—only more so, because He is not merely God's offspring. He is God Himself: "the radiance of the glory of God and the exact imprint of his nature" (Heb. 1:3). When we observe Jesus and His ways, we not only see hints and abstractions of God's nature; we actually see God at work.

"Whoever has seen me has seen the Father," Jesus said (John 14:9). Jesus reveals God. He makes Him known and knowable to us.

Second, *Jesus' deity exalts Him above all others.*

We've done a lot in our generation to emphasize the humanity of Jesus, to make Him feel more accessible and "down to earth." And truly He is our friend, our brother, One who can intimately understand and relate to us. But even in drawing as near to Him as He invites us to do, we must remember that His full understanding of our humanity comes from His deity. More than being merely human, He is transcendent. He is greater than any human who's ever lived because He is unique among all who've ever lived.

Most important, *Jesus' deity affirms Him as the exclusive way to God.*

If Jesus is not divine, He is only a man, and we are as

foolish and idolatrous in worshiping Him as if we chose to worship anyone else. If Jesus were not God in flesh, He could not be the "the way, and the truth, and the life" (John 14:6). He could not be our sole reliable path to God because there would *be* no path to God.

Is it *intolerant* to believe Jesus is God? To live by this belief and put our hope in it? If it is . . . so be it. We don't come to this belief because we choose it, but because it is true. And because it is true, here we take our stand, and herein is our only hope in this life and the next.

{ *Prayer* }

Lord, I declare in confident faith what You have both said and shown to be true about Yourself, and I accept You as my rightful Lord and King. May no other gods be given a place on the throne of my heart. By Your Holy Spirit, continually guide me into truth wherever I am confronted with compromise and empower me to obey You as one who believes You are the one true and living God.

{ Keep Reading }

EXODUS 20:1–6

"You shall have no other gods before me." (v. 3)

PSALM 89:5–8

"Who in the skies can be compared to the Lord?" (v. 6)

JOHN 10:31–38

"The Father is in me and I am in the Father." (v. 38)

{ Consider }

How do the implications of Jesus' deity affect you personally today? How do they answer a mindset, pattern, temptation, or doubt that you find to be troubling?

DECEMBER 11

THE WAITING

Great indeed, we confess, is the mystery of godliness.

{ 1 TIMOTHY 3:16 }

ONE OF THE GREAT DELIGHTS of the Christmas season, of course, is experiencing it through the eyes of children. Their squealing sense of excitement and anticipation takes us back to those days when we were children ourselves, enduring the slow passage of time until Christmas morning.

I suppose we all can remember what it was like to be mystified by a certain package under the tree that looked nothing like the size or shape of anything we'd asked for or expected to receive. What *was* it? We couldn't tell. We wanted to know, but no one would say. Picking it up or even shaking it could never give sufficient clues to satisfy our mounting curiosity. We just had to wait. And waiting for mystery to be revealed can be the longest waiting of all.

When we consider the mystery of Jesus' nature—fully God and yet also fully human (as we'll begin looking at tomorrow and continue for the next few days), we're inevitably left with questions that cannot be answered to our complete understanding. The Scriptures give us a lot of information and insight into who He is, with His Spirit opening our eyes to see and understand the contents of this living Word. But still we must end many days by setting down our Bibles like one of those tantalizing Christmas presents and accepting the mystery as part of the package. In all our desire to know and understand, we must learn to be comfortable in not yet knowing.

The secular world sees this admission on our part as a cop-out. They say that if we can't entirely explain Jesus—if not even His own followers can give acceptable answers to every question—how can what we claim really be true? But if we could somehow encapsulate the awe and wonder of Jesus into a little box to be perfectly measured and processed and stamped with our human seal of approval, then He wouldn't be so amazing anymore. He wouldn't be God enough to do what His Word says He has done and is continuing to do.

A morning is coming—a new and endless morning—when our eyes will awaken to glories and beauties and the light of eternal realities that will wipe every question of Jesus' identity from the blackboard of mystery. We'll see and know. We'll hold Him and worship Him. We'll stand in His presence among our blood-washed family of the redeemed, and we'll know beyond knowing that this gift—this unspeakable gift—was worth every hour of waiting.

Must we live with mystery now? Oh, yes. But if the mystery

is this "great," as Scripture says, just imagine the greatness of His total revealing.

{ *Prayer* }

I bend low before You today, Lord, in worship and adoration. You who owe us nothing have delighted in showing us enough of Your glory already to be stunned by how vast and great You are. Help me praise and honor you now, as I will wish I had done when I behold You face to face. I ask it in Jesus' matchless name.

{ *Keep Reading* }

JOB 28:20–28

"God understands the way to it." (v. 23)

PSALM 68:15–20

"The chariots of God are twice ten thousand." (v. 17)

HEBREWS 9:24–28

"To save those who are eagerly waiting for him." (v. 28)

{ *Consider* }

How do you tend to live with mystery in your life? What makes the difference in whether the unknowns about God that remain in your mind move you toward doubt or toward greater faith?

Jesus
HIS CHOSEN HUMANITY

Christ Jesus,
who, though he was in the form of God,
did not count equality with God a thing to be grasped,
but emptied himself, by taking the form of a servant,
being born in the likeness of men.

{ PHILIPPIANS 2:5–7 }

DECEMBER 12

DOUBLE PRIZES

When the fullness of time had come,
God sent forth his Son, born of woman, born under
the law, to redeem those who were under the law.

{ GALATIANS 4:4-5 }

IF YOU'VE EVER HAD TROUBLE AGREEING with a friend about where to go for dinner, imagine the task awaiting hundreds of staunchly opinionated bishops from every corner of the known world in the fifth century of the Christian era, trying to agree on how best to explain who Jesus is.

The first three or four hundred years of Christian history following Jesus' return to heaven were largely taken up with solving controversies related to His nature and identity. Heresies arose, gathering adherents and momentum. One camp said He was God but not man. Another group said that He was man but not God. Still others insisted that He was somewhere in the middle, a mingling of half and half.

It was troubling. Confusing. And *crucial*—because if Jesus is not God, He has no power and authority to save us, and if

Jesus is not human, the sacrifice of His death and triumph of His resurrection lose their meaning. All our hopes for eternity need Him to be both. He *must* be both, or else we are not saved.

To address important controversies like this, church leaders began gathering in a series of worldwide councils. At the fourth of these, held in the city of Chalcedon (in modern-day Turkey), the gathered religious leaders hammered out a creed supported by four foundational pillars: (1) Christ is fully God, (2) Christ is fully human, (3) His divine and human natures are not the same, (4) His divine and human natures are completely united in one person.

No council could ever explain, of course, exactly how God did all this. And yet the framers of the Chalcedonian Creed wisely let these biblical truths hang there in tension:

One hundred percent God; one hundred percent human. Not two different beings; one and the same.

The paradox—the mystery—of Jesus' nature is something we must still grapple with today as we encounter Him in Scripture. We see Him at the wedding in Cana, for example—a regular guest like all the others, except in one particular: He could turn water into wine. We see Him tired enough to fall asleep in the well of a boat on the Sea of Galilee, and yet able upon being awakened to silence a howling windstorm with a single utterance.

God. Man.

Jesus.

Satan does not want us to engage with this paradox, to grasp who Jesus really is. The enemy's mission depends on keeping Jesus small enough in our minds that He can't truly be effective at helping us and satisfying us. But like the believers of old, when we hear erroneous ideas spouted that minimize Christ's nature and ability, we must keep going back to the Word, repeating to ourselves what the Bible affirms to be true:

His humanity makes Him *willing* to save us. His divinity makes Him *able* to save us.

Willing. Able.

Jesus.

{ *Prayer* }

Father, as I consider the mystery of Jesus as
revealed in Your Word, it becomes clear that
He is more than I could possibly know.
Thank You for sending Your Son to this earth,
into the most hopeless situation known to man,
to do a job that required nothing less than
a God-Man. I worship You today for the fullness
of these gifts You've given for my sins,
for my salvation, in Jesus' name.

{ *Keep Reading* }

PSALM 80:1–3

"Stir up your might
and come to save us!" (v. 2)

MICAH 7:8–9

"He will bring me out to the light." (v. 9)

HEBREWS 7:23–28

"He is able to save to the uttermost." (v. 25)

{ *Consider* }

Think of a desire in your life that you feel willing but not able to fulfill—or able but not willing. How do these parallels help you clarify both Jesus' power and His heart when it comes to the work of redemption?

DECEMBER 13

CAREFUL WITH THE BABY

Take care, and keep your soul diligently,
lest you forget the things that your eyes have seen.

{ DEUTERONOMY 4:9 }

PERHAPS WE COULD CALL IT the "Away in a Manger" effect. Remember those words from the familiar carol:

> The cattle are lowing, the Baby awakes,
> But little Lord Jesus, no crying He makes.[4]

I've been around lots of babies in my time. And, yes, each one is adorable and precious. But let's just acknowledge what we all know to be true when it comes to babies: *crying they make!* The idea that Jesus, when he "laid down his sweet head," might have caused the hay on which He slept to glisten in the light of His halo is a function of medieval art, not at all a picture of reality.

Jesus was conceived in the physical womb of a physical

young woman. He was born on earth as a baby at an actual historical time in an actual geographical place—"born in the likeness of men," as the Bible puts it (Phil. 2:7). Five times in the second chapter of Luke alone, the Gospel writer refers to Him as a "child." A child who grew and matured as children do, who "increased in wisdom and in stature and in favor with God and man" (Luke 2:52). And a child who surely made more than a peep in His infant crib.

I hope you don't hear all this as a swipe at a beloved Christmas hymn, a lullaby as lovely as any ever written. We can sing it and worship the Lord with it as we do with other favorite carols. But it does provide a good object lesson for how easily and innocently we can absorb beliefs into our system without checking them for biblical accuracy . . . and how the Christmas season, with all its mingling of cultural and sentimental mythologies, can be fertile ground for this tendency.

It's worth mentioning again that Jesus' coming as a human being was primarily a salvation event. It was the visible emergence of God's eternal plan to rescue His people from their sins—a plan that required the Son to take on a physical body and live an earthly life. In order for Him to make full atonement for our sins by His own blood, He had to first *become* flesh and blood. The Lamb that was slain needed first to be a little baby, one who could shed real tears, make real cries.

We know that "in the days of his flesh, Jesus offered up prayers and supplications, with loud cries and tears" to His

Father in heaven (Heb. 5:7)—the way *we* do, the way *we* should do. Why would it not stand to reason that He could burst forth with "loud cries and tears" as a baby, just as we did?

{ *Prayer* }

Lord, help me stay open to everything You show me in Your Word—everything You reveal that demands my complete trust and obedience. But help me also to be alert to anything I hear in other places, no matter how right sounding and good feeling, that does not line up with Your truth. May I live before You worshipfully; before the world, watchfully.

{ *Keep Reading* }

PSALM 25:4–5

"Lead me in your truth and teach me." (v. 5)

JEREMIAH 23:26–29

"Let him who has my word speak my word faithfully." (v. 28)

2 TIMOTHY 4:1–5

"As for you, always be sober-minded." (v. 5)

{ *Consider* }

What are some inconsistencies between the Christian celebration of Christmas and the secular? How can you successfully separate truth from fiction?

DECEMBER 14

THE HUMAN CONDITION

Since therefore the children share in flesh and blood, he himself likewise partook of the same things.

{ HEBREWS 2:14 }

EACH OF US FACES MULTIPLE DECISIONS EVERY DAY. And as they come to us one by one and we respond, we are essentially deciding, moment by moment, whether or not we are going to be like Jesus.

But Jesus, in choosing His ministry on the earth, chose every day to be like *us* in our humanity.

"Is not this the carpenter's son?" people would ask at times, when something about Him suggested He was Someone special (Matt. 13:55). "Is not this Jesus, the son of Joseph, whose father and mother we know?"

To the people of His day, Jesus looked like just an ordinary man. He did normal human things. He wore normal human clothes. He ate, He drank, He breathed our air.

Jesus also confined Himself to our everyday physical

limitations and weaknesses. As an unfallen man, He would have experienced various constraints and realities that are part of being human. For instance, He walked from place to place; He didn't fly around like Superman. The Scripture specifically makes mention of times when He grew tired and sought rest. We see Him wearied at times from His work and His traveling. He became hungry when He went without food for too long. He got thirsty, as He said from the cross, when He was denied adequate hydration. We also know that He suffered physical pain. Scripture says, "He had to be made like his brothers in every respect" (Heb. 2:17).

Bottom line: Jesus came to earth to be like *us*. Not only was He physically human, but He also had a human makeup and soul. He possessed all the elements we understand and experience as being parts of our human nature. Whatever it means to be a human being, apart from sin, Jesus had it. Jesus lived it.

Why?

So that we could truly—finally—live like *Him*.

Apart from Jesus, we are sinners without hope of ever changing our spots. Even our best attempts at living righteously are akin to what Isaiah famously called "filthy rags" (Isa. 64:6 NKJV). But because Jesus came as one of us, yet succeeded at living as none of us can do, we can now say with Paul, "It is no longer I who live, but Christ who lives in me" (Gal. 2:20). Jesus went to the cross and suffered as a *human*. In so doing, He fulfilled this powerful promise: "What is impossible with man is possible with God" (Luke 18:27).

{ *Prayer* }

Lord, I desire to be more like You—in my thinking, in my relationships, in my work and my leisure, in all my living. But I know the only reason this is possible is because Jesus Himself came to be like me and to take the penalty I deserved for my sin. Where I struggle, teach me how to simply trust that You will provide what you have promised—all I need for life and godliness, in Jesus' name.

{ *Keep Reading* }

PSALM 18:31–34

"He made my feet like the feet of a deer." (v. 33)

HAGGAI 2:4–5

"Work, for I am with you." (v. 4)

COLOSSIANS 1:24–29

"Christ in you, the hope of glory." (v. 27)

{ *Consider* }

How do your physical experiences impact you spiritually—aches and pains, susceptibility to fatigue, various limitations? What difference does it make to you that Jesus truly understands these experiences?

DECEMBER 15

KNOWING HOW IT FEELS

Humble yourselves, therefore . . . casting all your anxieties on him, because he cares for you.

{ 1 PETER 5:6–7 }

WE ARE ALL EMOTIONAL BEINGS. (Don't we know it!) And perhaps by this time in the Christmas season—just ten days until the big day—you're feeling these emotions a bit more. They could be feelings of panic and pressure, the sense of being overwhelmed by all that remains undone. They could be feelings of sadness and emptiness, spawned by certain changes or losses in your life that cause your heart to sag more at Christmas than at other times. They could even involve a mix of happy anticipating and dread—a complex mix of emotional ups and downs involving expectation, memory, hope, fear, and gratitude.

Whatever emotions you're experiencing this season, remember that because Jesus fully relates to us on a human level, He relates to our emotions too. He understands them. After all, He was an emotional being as well.

He cared for outcast lepers and for needy multitudes, for a widow who'd just lost her son.

He marveled at things like the unblinking faith placed in Him by a tough Roman centurion.

He rejoiced at the opportunity to bring hope and healing to hurting people.

He grieved at the tomb of His friend Lazarus, at the thought of Jerusalem rejecting her Messiah, and at the Last Supper with His closest circle of friends, where He was "troubled in his spirit" (John 13:21).

He even grew angry at the hypocritical religious leaders and the opportunistic merchants defiling the temple.

The only difference between Jesus' emotions and ours, in fact, was in how He handled them. We're prone to squander our emotions on the wrong things, to let them spill out uncontrollably, to let them take the lead in our responses and decision-making rather than supporting our true convictions.

Jesus, however—though acquainted with all the ways we're tempted to overreact—always expressed His emotions in a wholesome, balanced, godly way. And because of the righteous alignment of His heart, He was moved to emotion most by those things that moved the heart of God.

All of this is instructive . . . and incredibly encouraging. You and I, in seeking to be conformed to the likeness of Christ, need not squelch or bury our emotions. We need not choke them back into heartburn, restraining them with clenched fists of denial. Emotions are not inherently *wrong*; if they were, the man Jesus would not have experienced or expressed them. Even as we feel them rising today at the nearness of Christmas, whether in exasperation or elation, we need only submit them to His sovereignty, not stuff them into shame-filled pockets of inadmissible pain or guilty pleasure.

Jesus was no dry-eyed, joyless, unfeeling robot. He knows what it's like to hurt, to laugh, to wish, to agonize. And He knows how to be your comfort and companion when you experience the same.

{ *Prayer* }

Thank You, Father, for not sending Jesus to us as Someone who couldn't feel. Thank You for not steeling His nerve endings against our hard, unforgiving world, but rather allowing Him to experience stress at levels that far surpass my own. I ask You, Lord Jesus, to take control of my runaway emotions, showing me how to fully feel them without becoming consumed or misdirected by them.

{ *Keep Reading* }

PSALM 116:8–14

"I believed, even when I spoke:
'I am greatly afflicted.'" (v. 10)

ISAIAH 38:17–20

"Behold, it was for my welfare
that I had great bitterness." (v. 17)

JOHN 12:23–27

"Now is my soul troubled. And what shall I say?" (v. 27)

{ *Consider* }

Where are your emotions today?
What about Jesus could help give perspective
to your feelings?

DECEMBER 16

FIRST CUT

At the end of eight days, when he was circumcised,
he was called Jesus,
the name given by the angel
before he was conceived in the womb.

{ LUKE 2:21 }

WE DON'T KNOW MANY DETAILS of Jesus' childhood. Some wrongly imagine Him a young wizard, based on nonbiblical stories that show Him performing various miracles—saving his brother from a snakebite, bringing clay birds to life, and so on. But we need none of this false narrative to know all we need to know about Jesus as a boy—including a pivotal scene, often overlooked as a passing comment, in Luke 2:21. We are told that the infant Jesus was circumcised when he was eight days old.

The practice of circumcision, we know, had been given to Abraham in Genesis 17 as the sign and seal of God's covenant with the Jewish people. All Jewish males at eight days of age were required to undergo this procedure, and by the time Jesus was born, Jewish parents had been circumcising their infant boys for thousands of years.

Circumcision was much more, however, than an early form of nonelective surgery. Even as far back as the days of Moses, people understood it as representing a "circumcision of the heart." That is, it was a physical reminder that they as fallen people were to separate themselves from their sins—to actually cut them away.

But Jesus, unlike other human males, had no sins that needed removal. He was sinless. He was perfect. What then did *His* circumcision mean? Why did God's own Son have to endure a sensitive, serious cut He didn't need, either on His body or His heart?

Two reasons.

First, Jesus' parents were ensuring that their newborn fulfilled the law's requirements. Even as a child too young to be responsible for his actions, Jesus is shown in Scripture as obeying this command, doing what Jewish newborns do. He would never have been recognized as the Son of David, the seed of Abraham—the Messiah in their midst—had He not been one of their own, even in this severing of His flesh.

But then beautifully, redemptively, Jesus' circumcision also foretells His suffering, His willingness to shed His own innocent blood. It was only a few drops at this point, but this procedure was already a picture of the blood that would one day flow down His body as He paid the staggering price for your sins and mine.

And so against whatever cloth or wrapping Jesus lay upon

when His skin felt its first incision, we see a faint shadow of the cross. We see Him as a baby, barely a week old, submitting Himself to an ordinance needed not for Himself, but for others. For us. This child who had no sins to be cut away was already suffering sin's consequences.

It's one of the reasons why He needed to be made in human likeness. It's why His humanity matters as much as His divinity. It is why He came. And it is once again why we worship Him as we consider Jesus this Christmas.

{ *Prayer* }

Thank You for Your written Word, Lord—
so rich in detail, so interwoven in unity. Thank
You for this incredible plan that we celebrate at
Christmas, but that also overflows its banks to
fill each day of the year with wonder, provision,
and worship. In this Advent season, I'm filled with
joy at being forgiven by One who needed no
forgiveness Himself. Hallelujah.

{ Keep Reading }

GENESIS 17:10–14

"He who is eight days old among you shall be circumcised." (v. 12)

PSALM 22:22–24

"He has not despised or abhorred the affliction of the afflicted." (v. 24)

COLOSSIANS 2:11–14

"In him also you were circumcised." (v. 11)

{ Consider }

In these past days of pondering Jesus' deity and His humanity, what discoveries have you found most refreshing and revealing? Which have brought you to fresh worship and gratitude?

Jesus

HIS EARTHLY EXAMPLE

For we do not have a high priest who is unable
to sympathize with our weaknesses,
but one who in every respect has been
tempted as we are, yet without sin.

{ HEBREWS 4:15 }

DECEMBER 17

ONE DOWN

Who is like the LORD our God,
Who dwells on high,
Who humbles Himself to behold
The things that are in the heavens and in the earth?

{ PSALM 113:5–6 NKJV }

FATHER DAMIEN WAS A YOUNG BELGIAN PRIEST who left his homeland in the 1800s to journey to a remote village on the Hawaiian island of Molokai. Not a bad option, you'd think, as a choice of ministry location. People need Jesus in Hawaii, too, and Hawaii then, as now, was a beautiful place to live!

Actually, though, no one had thus far been willing to accept the assignment to this particular obscure outpost. It was a government-imposed quarantine area for victims of what is now called Hansen's disease but then was known as leprosy.

Father Damien had been assigned to a leper colony—to live and work with victims of what was at the time an incurable and wasting disease.

For sixteen years, Father Damien labored among the suffering outcasts of Molokai, learning their language, leading construction projects, organizing improvements to their living conditions. Rather than being repulsed at making physical contact with his flock, he ate with them, embraced them, gave them the dignity of interacting with them. Over time their community was transformed into a place of hope and opportunity. Mind, body, and soul, people began to thrive and experience joy in living.

One Lord's Day ten years or so into his ministry, Father Damien stood before his congregation and in two words summarized the dedication of his life to this cause. In speaking of the daily struggles his parishioners endured, he pointedly referred both to them and himself as "we lepers." Father Damien, after living hand to hand among those with this wasting disease, had become a leper himself.

At Christmas we ponder the unthinkable, the unimaginable. God has come into our pitiful, putrid village. He has become one of us. This One who must humble Himself to even "behold the things that are in the *heavens*"—imagine that!—has stooped immeasurably further. If even the glories of heaven are a step down from what He had been experiencing at each divine moment of His eternal existence, picture Him choosing to come and live here among our dust and grime and smells and pollution . . . with us lepers.

Feel today what David felt when pondering the mysteries of God's condescension:

> When I look at your heavens, the work of your fingers,
> the moon and the stars, which you have set in place,
> what is man that you are mindful of him,
> and the son of man that you care for him?
> (Psalm 8:3–4)

We look up, but Jesus looked down . . . not only to *see* us but to *be* us, to live like us and to make His home with us. He stooped down to love us, to be near us, to rub shoulders with us, to be one of us. To know us and care for us.

The lepers on Molokai never viewed Father Damien the same way after he admitted in words and then evidenced in flesh his complete identification with them in their diseased state. This man who had come to live with them would now also die like them.

"We lepers" have a new Brother among us. And we have all of this season to consider it, to celebrate Him.

{ *Prayer* }

Lord, Your condescension falls on me today with fresh weight and amazement. Every moment of prideful self-importance I've ever entertained now brings me to my knees in worship for what You gave up to be my Savior. Thanks is not enough, and yet You even humble Yourself enough to be blessed by my gratitude. I honor and bless You for humbling Yourself for the likes of sinners such as I.

{ *Keep Reading* }

PSALM 102:18–22

"He looked down from his holy height." (v. 19)

ISAIAH 66:1–2

"This is the one to whom I will look: he who is humble." (v. 2)

ROMANS 12:14–18

"Do not be haughty, but associate with the lowly." (v. 16)

{ *Consider* }

How could you actively choose this Christmas
to reach "down" to those who are needy,
as Jesus reached down to meet you in your need?
How can you do this with humility rather than
in a condescending spirit?

DECEMBER 18

NAMING RIGHTS

You made him for a little while lower than the angels.

{ HEBREWS 2:7 }

ONE OF THE PASSAGES you've probably heard read this season and will likely be hearing again as you enter this final week before Christmas is the Matthew 1 account of the angel appearing to Joseph in a dream, confirming his prior message to Mary. She indeed was pregnant—not by any man but by the Holy Spirit—and would soon bear a son, whom Joseph was instructed to name Jesus. Then, at the close of the chapter, you read these simple, obedient words: "*And he called his name Jesus*" (v. 25).

In hearing that name repeated—Jesus ("Yahweh saves"[5])—our heart instantly registers both its strength and precious beauty. Which we should! Praise His name! But in this quiet Advent moment today, pause to recognize something else that is mentioned less explicitly—implied more than stated.

Not only does Jesus' *name* have meaning. The fact that He was named *at all* has meaning.

Scroll back in your biblical memory all the way to the beginning, where Scripture reports God bringing to Adam all the various types of birds and beasts He had made. "*Whatever the man called every living creature*," says Genesis 2:19, "*that was its name*." This naming of the animals builds on what God had said in Genesis 1 about giving humankind "dominion" over all other aspects of creation.

To be given a name, in other words, implies that you allow someone else to exercise dominion over you. It reflects submission to authority.

Let's remember that Jesus the Son is from above, dwelling in heavenly places, "far above all rule and authority and power and dominion, and above every name that is named, not only in this age but also in the one to come" (Eph. 1:21). Remember, too, that "at the name of Jesus every knee will bow, of those who are in heaven and on earth and under the earth, and that every tongue will confess that Jesus Christ is Lord, to the glory of God the Father" (Phil. 2:10–11 NASB).

That's who Jesus is—incredibly, eternally, exclusively powerful above every created being in heaven and earth. And yet He submitted Himself to the human practice of being given a name. This One "from whom every family in heaven and on earth is named" (Eph. 3:15) bowed Himself low enough to be given a name common to His historical era, a version of the Hebrew name *Yeshua*, or *Joshua*. He who holds all dominion and authority allowed an earthy, nondescript carpenter to "call his name Jesus."

Remarkable.

Stand back in amazement today at this wonderful truth: the Son, though equal with the Father, willingly submitted Himself to the Father's authority. He who created all things— of whom it is accurately said, "Without him was not any thing made that was made" (John 1:3)—willingly placed Himself in a position of receiving.

It's a level of submission beyond words. Unless that word is . . . *Jesus*.

{ *Prayer* }

Lord, I exalt Your name. You are worthy of every praise, greater than all my imagining of Your grandeur. And yet I find myself today exalting You for Your willingness to come down from Your heights of glory, to be made "for a little while lower than the angels." Had You not done that, I would still be lost in my sins. Since You did, I can make my prayer "in Jesus' name."

{ *Keep Reading* }

PSALM 89:25–28

"He shall cry to me, 'You are my Father.'" (v. 26)

ISAIAH 49:1–3

"From the body of my mother he named my name." (v. 1)

JOHN 8:52–55

"It is my Father who glorifies me." (v. 54)

{ *Consider* }

In what relationship or area of your life
might you feel entitled to assert your will
and dominance over another this Christmas?
How does Jesus' example call you to surrender
any sense of entitlement?

DECEMBER 19

FOOD FIGHT

"It is written,
'Man shall not live by bread alone,
but by every word that comes from the mouth of God.'"

{ MATTHEW 4:4 }

IT'S SAFE TO SAY, I BELIEVE, that no other holiday is so readily identified with food as Christmas. Thanksgiving, of course, is a close second, yet its favorite tastes and dishes are generally confined to a single day's meal (followed, of course, by the plentiful leftovers). Christmas, though, with all its customary gatherings and childhood memories, can lend itself to weeks of opportunities for sugary indulgences, rich hors d'oeuvres, and sumptuous meals.

I'm guessing, then, that you understand the common Christmas feeling of being full but still wanting to eat. (I'm not judging, you understand. I'm *relating*!) And while we may at times feel justified in partaking of an extra helping or two of seasonal delights, the fact remains that such indulgence is often simply our flesh wanting to have its own way. We want what we want, and we don't want to be told that we can't or that we shouldn't.

The enemy, when tempting Jesus in the wilderness (Matt. 4:1–11), appealed first to His physical appetites. Jesus, you may recall, hadn't eaten in nearly a month and a half. He could not have been human and completely avoided the idea that after forty days He deserved permission to break His fast. But His battle that day, though obviously different from our Christmas struggles in the extreme, still hinged around the same issue as when we ponder whether to stop by the pantry on the way to bed tonight.

It's the issue of *Who's in charge here?*

It's the question of *Will I surrender to God's lordship in my life, or will I insist on running things myself?*

By the time we see Jesus in Gethsemane, praying those earnest, heartfelt words, "Not my will, but yours, be done" (Luke 22:42), we're witnessing fruit from an entire life of complete, glad, wholehearted, consistent surrender to His Father. As awe-inspiring as His willingness to endure the cross sounds, it actually just follows the trajectory He'd set with each day He lived on the earth.

"The Son can do nothing of his own accord," Jesus said early in His ministry, "but only what he sees the Father doing. For whatever the Father does, that the Son does likewise" (John 5:19). "I have come down from heaven," He later told His disciples, "not to do my own will but the will of him who sent me" (John 6:38). He elaborated on this theme again and again: "I do as the Father has commanded me" (John 14:31). "I always do the things that are pleasing to him" (John 8:29).

Our question around the snack table at this week's Christmas party or family get-together is really the question that should govern every moment of every day. *Who makes the call? Who gets to say? Who do we allow to win this battle of wills?*

Jesus doesn't make it easy, but He does make it simple. We are to remain obediently surrendered, walking in step with the Word and the Spirit of God.

{ *Prayer* }

Dear heavenly Father, I know that the desires
You have given me flow from Your goodness.
You intend them to lead me to blessing,
to enable me to find my joy and satisfaction
in You. Help me not to be persuaded by
my own or my enemy's logic, but to gladly say
"yes" to You, knowing that will result in what is
truly best for me. I choose You both now and
always. In the all-sufficient name of Jesus.

{ Keep Reading }

PSALM 63:3–8

"My soul will be satisfied as with fat and rich food." (v. 5)

ISAIAH 50:7–10

"The Lord God helps me;
therefore I have not been disgraced." (v. 7)

1 JOHN 3:19–24

"We keep his commandments and do what pleases him." (v. 22)

{ Consider }

Where are you most feeling the battle today between your will and God's? Who will win? Which choice, if you made it right now, would declare your surrender to Him?

DECEMBER 20

HUMILITY

Take my yoke upon you, and learn from me,
for I am gentle and lowly in heart,
and you will find rest for your souls.

{ MATTHEW 11:29 }

HUMILITY WAS NOT CONSIDERED A VIRTUE in ancient Greco-Roman ethics. The closest the Latin and Greek vocabulary came to expressing this quality was a word we translate into English as "lowly." But even then the concept equated to being cowardly or timid. It was viewed as a vice or a failing, not a virtue.

Meekness, in other words, meant weakness to the first-century mind. Humility was not championed, even hypocritically, by those who assumed places of leadership and influence in their government, their religion, and their community life.

Against that backdrop, Jesus' teaching on the subject and His own example of it would have been viewed as nothing short of revolutionary in His day.

We're familiar, of course, with the many examples from

the Gospels where leaders of Jewish society rejected Jesus as their Messiah. We think we understand this reaction—how He didn't fit the expected role of a dashing military conqueror, come to pay back in their oppressors' blood the wrongs done to their nation, setting Israel up again as a dominant world power.

But we probably can never grasp from our historical vantage point how vastly different this carpenter's son appeared from the messianic imagery his fellow Jews had carried around in their heads all their lives. For Jesus to elevate humility into something positive and desirable clashed like plaids and stripes with the aspirations their culture had built into them.

And Jesus didn't simply live and teach humility's importance as one of a cluster of godly character traits; He rightly understood it as the root of every virtue. Just as human pride had been and continued to be the root of every sin, just as pride had severed our relationship with God going all the way back to the garden of Eden, humility was presented by Jesus as foundational to reversing what had been lost in the Fall.

"Lowly in heart" is how Jesus accurately described Himself. "Blessed are the meek, for they shall inherit the earth" is how He measured humility's value (Matt. 5:5).

"He who is least among you all is the one who is great," He taught His followers (Luke 9:48) in absolutely upside-down, totally backward fashion from what they'd always thought and experienced.

And the cross, for all the ways we try capturing it in thought and word, is the living and dying epitome of humility in action.

Jesus, if He had been remotely interested in boasting, would make our loudest human boasting sound like the reedy chirping of a distant songbird. Instead, He revealed His greatness by the greatness of His humility. In the words of South African pastor and writer Andrew Murray more than a century ago, "His humility is our salvation. His salvation is our humility."[6] The humility of Jesus, he said, "is the secret, the hidden root of thy redemption."[7]

{ *Prayer* }

I continue to marvel at what I see in You,
Lord Jesus. Your vastness, Your greatness—
they are more than my heart and mind can hold.
But to see You living out such humility from
cradle to the grave astounds me even more.
Show me how to embrace and embody this virtue
from the inside out, as I seek to become
more like You in every way.

{ Keep Reading }

PSALM 34:1–3

"My soul makes its boast in the LORD." (v. 2)

ZEPHANIAH 3:11–13

"I will leave in your midst
a people humble and lowly." (v. 12)

LUKE 14:7–11

"He who humbles himself will be exalted." (v. 11)

{ Consider }

How does the humility of Jesus reveal His greatness? How does it speak to our natural pride and self-seeking? How can considering Him bring us to a place of greater humility?

DECEMBER 21

YOU CAN DO THIS

We do not have a high priest who is unable to sympathize with our weaknesses, but one who in every respect has been tempted as we are, yet without sin.

{ HEBREWS 4:15 }

ONE WHO IN EVERY RESPECT has been tempted as we are . . . That's how the author of Hebrews describes Jesus. Scripture says the temptations that feel the most pointed at us, the most personalized to us, are actually more "common to man" than we think (1 Cor. 10:13). In other words, we're not the only ones in the world dealing with these same issues. But to be able to "consider Jesus" in our moments of temptation is to know that not only is someone else across town feeling something like this, but even *Jesus* felt it. That's a powerful realization for you and for me.

But don't stop there. Finish the sentence.

". . . tempted as we are, *yet without sin*."

If we're not careful, we can transform the comfort of

knowing that Jesus understands our battles into a rationale for why He would surely understand if we gave in just this once. But to consider Jesus means to consider all of Him. And according to the Bible, Jesus doesn't just "sympathize with our weaknesses," He also can personally attest by His example that we are able to walk through them "without sin."

Jesus was fully God, as we've seen. But when He was here on earth, fulfilling His mission, He didn't rely on His powers as God to help Him overcome His human limitations. He still *retained* His divine power, of course, but He lived His perfectly sinless life as a man, as one of us. How? By doing what we can do. By depending on the Holy Spirit. Jesus used the same resources in defeating sin that are available to us today as human beings.

The same book of the Bible that attests, "God anointed Jesus of Nazareth with the Holy Spirit and with power" (Acts 10:38), also reports that Jesus said to His followers, "You will receive power when the Holy Spirit has come upon you" (Acts 1:8). So when you see Jesus loving unlovable people, you see Him doing it with the Spirit's power. When you see Him choosing to remain silent in the face of others' insults, He is doing it with the Spirit's power. In each of His reactions to the assault of both everyday and more intense temptations, you're seeing how you, too, can respond when faced with your own most powerful temptations.

Wrap your mind around that. Jesus has given you the Spirit that was given to Him.

The record of Jesus' earthly life is intended to be "an example, so that you might follow in [the] steps" of this One who "committed no sin, neither was deceit found in his mouth" (1 Peter 2:21–22). Not only has He shown you that He understands what it's like to face temptation; He has also shown you how to live "without sin."

Let's do it.

{ *Prayer* }

Thank You, Lord Jesus, for the example of your sinless life. Thank You for enduring a life in human flesh that You were under no obligation to experience so that we could see the way to overcome what our sinful hearts keep telling us is impossible. Thank You for sending Your Holy Spirit to be my strength and my reminder of truth—and to show me that sin is no longer the boss of me.

{ Keep Reading }

PSALM 145:14–19

"The Lord upholds all who are falling." (v. 14)

ISAIAH 51:1–3

"Look to the rock from which you were hewn." (v. 1)

1 JOHN 3:5–7

"He appeared in order to take away sins, and in him there is no sin." (v. 5)

{ Consider }

What would depending on the Holy Spirit have looked like when you were dealing with one of your most recent bouts with temptation? How could that mindset help you in your next bout with temptation?

Jesus
HIS MATCHLESS SUPREMACY

In these last days he has spoken to us by his Son,
whom he appointed the heir of all things,
through whom also he created the world.
He is the radiance of the glory of God and
the exact imprint of his nature,
and he upholds the universe by the word of his power.
After making purification for sins,
he sat down at the right hand of the Majesty on high.

{ HEBREWS 1:2–3 }

DECEMBER 22

HOW WONDERFUL

"Why do you ask my name, seeing it is wonderful?"

{ JUDGES 13:18 }

WONDERFUL IS ONE OF THOSE UMBRELLA WORDS we use that covers a wide range of specifics. When this holiday season is past, for instance, people will ask you, "How was your Christmas?" To which you might answer: "eventful," "delightful," "restful," "stressful," or "worshipful."

You might also say something like: "It was wonderful."

Wonderful covers a lot of ground.

Throughout this Advent walk together, we've found Jesus to be a lot of things. We've considered His cross, His deity, His humanity, His humility. We've seen His love and compassion, His power and glory. We could say so much, and all of it would be true. Each little slice of understanding, were we to delve deeper, would provide a spiritual feast of insight and truth. But "wonderful" serves us well as a shorthand way of communicating what could take forever to describe.

The nineteenth-century English preacher, writer, and

scholar Charles Spurgeon, preaching a series on the names of Jesus, took an uncommonly personal detour during one of those sermons, attempting to describe the reach and scope of Jesus' "wonderful" name.

Several years earlier, on a Sunday morning in 1856, while Spurgeon preached to a packed house of nearly fifteen thousand in Surrey Music Hall, someone in the audience shouted, "Fire!" Pandemonium ensued. People were trampled. Many were injured. Seven were killed.

In the aftermath of this tragedy, Spurgeon sank hard into the depression that had dogged him throughout his life, though perhaps never more savagely than now. Even his private practice of prayer, which once had been his anchor and solace in trouble, became too shrouded in fear and terror for him even to attempt.

One day, though, while walking alone in a friend's garden, seeking to sort out his dark thoughts, the simple name of Jesus registered in Spurgeon's mind. *Jesus*. Merely the name. And the wonder of that name struck him with full force. "I stood still," he recalled later. "The burning lava of my soul was cooled. My agonies were hushed. I bowed myself there, and the garden that had seemed a Gethsemane became to me a Paradise." Not even the prolifically gifted Spurgeon could come up with the right words to portray what he'd experienced in that moment, except to say, "His name has been from that time 'Wonderful' to me."[8]

Wonderful. Marvelous. Extraordinary. Beyond understanding. Bundle up all the remarkable, amazing things you know and hear and sense and imagine when you think on the name of Jesus. And if "wonderful" is all that comes out, it is wonderful enough indeed.

You may feel frustrated to the point of despair at times, unable to grasp all the things you wish to understand about Jesus. But if you were asked today to explain who He is, I think "wonderful" would please Him. *Wonderful* says a lot.

{ *Prayer* }

Lord, You are wonderful, more than I can imagine. You are everything I need. Forgive me for ever growing complacent in thinking on You and rehearsing to myself Your many acts and attributes. May nothing You have made, no matter how lovely and satisfying to my soul, rival my wonder over You alone, my Lord and my Savior.

{ Keep Reading }

JOB 42:1–6

"I know that you can do all things." (v. 2)

PSALM 9:1–2

"I will recount all of your wonderful deeds." (v. 1)

EPHESIANS 1:15–23

"[God] gave him as head over all things to the church." (v. 22)

{ Consider }

What have you found to be the most "wonderful" about this year's Christmas season?
How could you turn the joy you have experienced in those moments into fuel for your worship today?

DECEMBER 23

GREAT IN COUNSEL

This also comes from the LORD of hosts;
he is wonderful in counsel
and excellent in wisdom.

{ ISAIAH 28:29 }

IMAGINE NEVER HAVING AN UNANSWERED question—not because you always know how and where to find the answers, but because you already understand everything on your own. Imagine knowing exactly what to do at any given moment without ever needing to be told.

That's Jesus every day. He never experiences not knowing anything that can possibly be known. He needs no one for counsel. He is not only His own perfect counsel but also *our* perfect counselor. Our "Wonderful Counselor" (Isa. 9:6), wiser than all other earthly sources of wisdom put together.

In the days of King Solomon, who was known far and wide for the wisdom God had given him, the queen of Sheba came from her distant homeland to meet him. She wanted to see for herself if this legendary man was as wise as advertised—"to test him with hard questions" (1 Kings 10:1). The Bible says that she "told him all that was on her mind" (v. 2) and that Solomon responded masterfully to each inquiry. "There was nothing hidden from the king that he could not explain to her" (v. 3).

She left Jerusalem declaring that she had vastly underestimated the king. The depth of his counsel had completely overcome her skepticism. She was so overwhelmed after everything she'd seen and heard, in fact, that she was utterly speechless. Or, as the biblical writer puts it, "there was no more breath in her" (v. 5).

However, Jesus surpasses even this high bar set by the wise king. That obscure Old Testament queen had come "from the ends of the earth to hear the wisdom of Solomon," Jesus reminded His listeners (Matt. 12:42). But then He revealed what His audience that day and today's audience as well (you and I) need to know: "Behold, something greater than Solomon is here" (v. 42).

On our own, we can't always find the answers to the questions that nag and trouble us. Even the wise and knowledgeable people to whom we turn for guidance, however skilled, godly, and helpful they may be, are limited in the scope of what they can solve for us.

But we can seek counsel from the One who truly knows everything. We can trust the word of our Wonderful Counselor, whose wisdom and ways are without limit or flaw. We can communicate in prayer with Him at any hour of the day, resting in His full knowledge of Himself and of us. And even when we're left with unanswered questions, we can know without doubt that the answers are there, just waiting to be unfolded, in His own perfect timing. In the meantime, by spending time with Him, we continue growing in wisdom and understanding, until that day when we see Him "face to face" and we "shall know fully" (1 Cor. 13:12).

"Do not lean on your own understanding," as wise Solomon said (Prov. 3:5)—or on the understanding of any of the so-called Solomons of our age. Lean on "something greater," on your Wonderful Counselor.

{ *Prayer* }

I come to You today, Lord, with questions aplenty,
but with absolute confidence that none of these
mysteries bewilder You, that none of
my circumstances surprise You. Where Your Word
speaks to my needs directly, may I respond with
faith and obedience. And where my questions
perhaps require a lifetime of uncertainty,
settle me in knowing that You nevertheless
know all about it.

{ Keep Reading }

PSALM 73:21–26

"You guide me with your counsel." (v. 24)

JEREMIAH 32:17–19

"The LORD of hosts, great in counsel and mighty in deed." (vv. 18–19)

JUDE 24–25

"Now to him who is able to keep you from stumbling . . . be glory." (v. 24–25)

{ Consider }

Why might it be a good thing that we as humans do not know all there is to know? How can we get the answers and wisdom we need?

DECEMBER 24

FROM CREATOR TO CREATION

The Word became flesh and dwelt among us,
and we have seen his glory,
glory as of the only Son from the Father,
full of grace and truth.

{ JOHN 1:14 }

IN THE PREDAWN HOURS OF CHRISTMAS EVE 1968, three astronauts aboard the Apollo 8 spacecraft became the first humans to orbit the moon. Once they entered the moon's gravitational pull, they began an arc designed to orbit them around its never-before-seen "dark side." For thirty hair-raising minutes, the crew remained out of radio contact with the earth, until finally the commander's voice reemerged from the thick, crusty static to declare their circuit complete.

All day long the Apollo 8 crew continued making these two-hour revolutions until, at evening back in the States, they transmitted a live video message back to earth, estimated to be seen by more than a billion people around the world. As grainy, up-close images of the moon's surface flickered on TV screens, the astronauts took turns reading sections of the first ten verses of Genesis. They had visited the heavens and soon would be returning home.

If you weren't alive to experience this historic moment, it's hard to capture in words the triumph of that accomplishment, mingled with the thrill of hearing creation's story being read from hundreds of thousands of miles above our planet . . . on Christmas Eve, no less. But as astronaut James Irwin, who actually walked on the moon three years later, would observe after his return, "God walking on the earth is more important than man walking on the moon."[9]

The One who inhabited heaven's ivory palaces allowed Himself to be born of woman in a borrowed cattle shed. He who flung the stars into space made His lowly bed underneath them. The omniscient God humbled Himself to learn to walk and talk as a child; the eternal Word of God learned to read.

The One who fed His people with manna in the wilderness chose to become hungry. The Creator of oceans allowed Himself to experience thirst. He who never sleeps became weary. The great Helper of humankind became helpless and dependent.

Why?

"For God so loved the world, that he gave his only Son, that whoever believes in him should not perish but have eternal life" (John 3:16).

As you treasure this special, expectant day, whether alone or with your loved ones, as you close your eyes tonight on a year's worth of busyness and a lifetime's worth of Christmases, pause to marvel at what your Creator has done. Unwilling for you to remain enslaved any longer to sin and time and memories, He interrupted the unbroken rhythm of the calendar with a Christmas Eve for the ages. Bridging a distance far greater than the vast expanse between the earth and the moon, He did so much more than just leave us feeling nice and warm inside. He actually made it possible for us to become a new creation.

"Christ Jesus came into the world to save sinners" (1 Tim. 1:15). This is Christmas.

{ *Prayer* }

Father, on this Christmas Eve, You remind me of what I've known for years but too easily escapes me. Your Son's coming is not just a great happening amid other great happenings. It is everything. It is life itself. In the beauty of these hours, captivate my heart with the beauty of Your love and grace. Thank You for coming, Lord Jesus. Come again quickly.

{ Keep Reading }

GENESIS 1:1–10

"God said, 'Let there be light,' and there was light." (v. 3)

PSALM 18:4–10

"He bowed the heavens and came down." (v. 9)

ROMANS 8:31–32

"What then shall we say to these things?" (v. 31)

{ Consider }

Bring to your Christmas Eve this year
an Easter sense of joy that your Good Friday—
your long winter—is even now swallowed up
in victory. How might you put your worship
into words?

DECEMBER 25

STRONG AND SWEET

Your name is like perfume poured out.

{ SONG OF SOLOMON 1:3 NIV }

MERRY CHRISTMAS! As you join other Christ followers around the world in celebrating this holiday (holy-day), let's spend some time in simple contemplation of just how precious the name of Jesus is—and why.

First, crucially, His name is the source of our salvation. Not one of us—from the most loving and faithful Christian parent to the noblest and most eloquent pastor to the most altruistic and self-sacrificing soul—can save even one person. "There is salvation in no one else, for there is no other name under heaven given among men by which we must be saved" (Acts 4:12).

Undeniably, the name of Jesus is supreme. Many names from various fields of human endeavor rise to marquee level, known to their many thousands of fans and admirers as being the best at what they do. But not a single name from the world of music or film or athletics or politics is as gloriously everlasting as the name of Jesus.

To our great comfort, Jesus' name is strong and secure. Even amid the excitement and brightness of Christmas Day, you may be experiencing fears or concerns that you're trying to set aside for these blessed hours. Yet even if those nagging worries persist in intruding on your thoughts, remember:

> The name of the LORD is a strong tower;
> The righteous run to it and are safe. (Proverbs 18:10 NKJV)

And joy of joys, the name of Jesus is always sweet. Though it is saving in power, supreme in rank, strong in reliable protection, and totally secure in its endless duration, the name of Jesus remains sweet and delicious on the lips, soothing and peaceful on the heart. His name is indeed "like perfume poured out." And I hope the scent is evident at every turn in your home or wherever you may find yourself on this Christmas Day.

John Newton (1725–1827), the British slave trader turned Jesus lover and pastor, is best known for penning the hymn "Amazing Grace." Another of his hymns, though not a carol, expresses what's on my mind as we close this brief moment together today.

> How sweet the name of Jesus sounds
> In a believer's ear!
> It soothes his sorrows, heals his wounds,
> And drives away his fear. . . .

Dear name! the rock on which I build,
    My shield and hiding place,
My never-failing treas'ry, filled
    With boundless stores of grace;

Jesus, my Shepherd, Brother, Friend,
    My Prophet, Priest, and King,
My Lord, my Life, my Way, my End,
    Accept the praise I bring.[10]

{ *Prayer* }

How sweet is your name, Lord Jesus.
I lift it in praise to You today—the name that is
above every name. Thank You that I can run to the
safety and strength of Your name at all times,
in all situations, and will always find You
available to my need, valiant in my defense.
You are wonderful beyond words—yet may
my mouth be filled with words that express
my honor, love, and worship.

{ Keep Reading }

EXODUS 15:11–13

"You have guided them by your strength." (v. 13)

PSALM 104:33–34

"May my meditation be pleasing to him." (v. 34)

HEBREWS 13:14–15

"Let us continually offer up a sacrifice of praise . . . the fruit of lips that acknowledge his name." (v. 15)

{ Consider }

What have you experienced during this Advent season that has brought you closer to Christ? Who could you share this experience with before the new year?

Jesus

HIS ONGOING MINISTRY

He holds his priesthood permanently,
because he continues forever.
Consequently, he is able to save to the uttermost
those who draw near to God through him,
since he always lives to make intercession for them.

{ HEBREWS 7:24–25 }

DECEMBER 26

AFTER-CHRISTMAS SPECIALS

"My food is to do the will of him who sent me and to accomplish his work."

{ JOHN 4:34 }

SAD THAT CHRISTMAS IS OVER? Don't worry. It's not over. And I don't mean "it's not over" because you may still have family you're not visiting until this coming weekend, or because you're not due back at work until the new year, or maybe even because your tradition is to celebrate the twelve days of Christmas, which will keep you worshiping to a Christmas theme all the way through Epiphany on January 6.

What I mean by "Christmas isn't over" is that Jesus' work is not over. The incarnation is not merely a past-tense event. The impact of His coming to earth in flesh did not stop two thousand years ago when He returned to heaven, and it certainly won't stop because we've reached another annual milestone on the calendar!

We know from the biblical record that when Jesus appeared

to His followers in the aftermath of His resurrection, He was still present in bodily form. Yes, it was a *glorified* body that no longer retained the same restrictions He'd allowed Himself to accept from birth through His crucifixion. But people could see Him. They could touch Him. "See my hands and my feet," He said to them, "that it is I myself" (Luke 24:39).

Jesus ascended into heaven in that same glorified body. He still lives in that body today. And when He returns to earth a second time, those who are still making their home here will see Him in that resurrection body. "The Lord himself will descend from heaven" (1 Thess. 4:16)—still as God in flesh.

In other words, Jesus' body did not just vanish when He left our planet. Neither did His ministry end just because He so thoroughly, perfectly completed His mission of securing our salvation. To use a big Bible word, He had made "propitiation" for our sins (1 John 4:10), meaning He satisfied the righteous wrath of God against the evil in our hearts. He died the kind of death in our place that we deserved to die.

Even so, He sits today at the right hand of God, serving as our "advocate with the Father." "Jesus Christ the righteous" (1 John 2:1) presents Himself as sufficient evidence for why God's mercy should flow down and keep covering our sinful hearts. He serves, too, as our leading prayer warrior, since He "always lives to make intercession" for us as our great high priest (Heb. 7:25–26). He's not just hanging out in heaven, this God-Man.

So as you begin thinking about putting your Christmas things away, as the glow starts to fade from the long, exciting run-up to yesterday, remember that the incarnate babe in the manger has grown up but has not gone away. He still lives and works, still pleads for us and defends us.

Christmas is not over.

Christmas is never over.

{ *Prayer* }

Lord, thank You for continuing Your glorious
ministry even beyond the incomparable scenes
of Your cross and empty grave.
Your love for me extends through today
and into tomorrow, and it will never end.
May my love for You likewise stay strong and
grow stronger as I contemplate
just how much You have done and still do,
ever caring for Your people.

{ Keep Reading }

1 CHRONICLES 16:23–27

"Tell of his salvation from day to day." (v. 23)

PSALM 121:1–8

"He who keeps you will not slumber." (v. 3)

JOHN 17:24–26

"I made known to them your name, and I will continue to make it known." (v. 26)

{ Consider }

Who are you "making intercession" for today as the Christmas season winds down and another year begins? How are you continuing the work that Jesus came to do in and through you?

DECEMBER 27

MIGHTY CONFIDENT

"Behold, I am the LORD, the God of all flesh.
Is anything too hard for me?"

{ JEREMIAH 32:27 }

YOU'RE PROBABLY FAMILIAR with the great Christmas prophecy from Isaiah 9:6:

> For to us a child is born,
> to us a son is given;
> and the government shall be upon his shoulder,
> and his name shall be called
> . . . Mighty God. . . .

The original Hebrew term translated "Mighty God" is *El Gibbor*—*El* being the masculine noun for God, indicating His power and strength, and *Gibbor* meaning a warrior, a champion, a chief (translated elsewhere in some Bible versions as "mighty man of valor").

"Mighty God" was a name applied to Jesus centuries before He came to earth. And when His earthly ministry was complete, as He ascended into heaven, He affirmed that He would continue to be our Mighty God, the One we need for every exploit we attempt in obedience to His Word.

Before issuing His mandate to "go therefore and make disciples of all nations" (Matt. 28:19), Jesus said to His followers that they would not be left to themselves to break up the hard soil of people's hearts. Rather, "all authority in heaven and on earth has been given to me" (v. 18). He was sending them out with the ironclad confidence that their Mighty God was going ahead of them. There's nothing that He cannot do or has not done—and nothing that He cannot do through us.

One of the more dramatic appearances of *El Gibbor* in Scripture occurred when Jeremiah was serving as a prophet of God in Judah, not long before Babylon overpowered the Jewish people and dragged them into exile. By the time of Jeremiah 32, in fact, enemy forces were already erecting siege ramps around Jerusalem and cutting off essential supplies, prepared to sit it out while the city's inhabitants slowly starved.

Into this atmosphere—with defeat not a matter of if but when—the Lord instructed Jeremiah to do something that sounded absurd on the face of it. He told him to purchase a piece of local property, even as land values were plummeting. The Lord's intention was to communicate to His people that while things looked bad (*were* bad) at the moment, He was going to bring them back to their homeland at a divinely appointed time in their future.

The prophet did as he was told—agreed on terms, signed the papers, paid the money. He did this purely in obedience to God's command. He knew God had always fulfilled His word to His people in the past and that He was able to do what He had promised in this case: "Nothing is too hard for you. O great and mighty God"—*El Gibbor*—he prayed (Jer. 32:16–18).

But still, at the end of his prayer, he dared to wonder whether he had been sent on a fool's errand, given the fact that the city was to be given over to the Babylonians (v. 25).

God's reply was a rhetorical question, reminding His servant of what he already knew to be true: "Is anything too hard for me?" (v. 27).

Is anything too hard for *El Gibbor*? That's a question for you to ask today about any challenge you may be facing. Is anything too hard for your Mighty God?

El Gibbor is still on the job, and *El Gibbor* will do all He has promised.

Trust Him. Follow Him. Obey Him. And just watch what happens next!

{ Prayer }

You are the Mighty God. You hold all power and have no limits. The whole world, though it may seem to be falling apart around us, is under Your control. You can do anything. So I trust You today enough to follow Your Word and say yes to Your Spirit, knowing You will do what You have said.

{ Keep Reading }

DEUTERONOMY 10:12–22

"The great, the mighty, and the awesome God." (v. 17)

PSALM 20:6–8

"We trust in the name of the Lord our God." (v. 7)

REVELATION 15:2–4

"Great and amazing are your deeds." (v. 3)

{ Consider }

What actions are you hesitating to take—actions you know to be in keeping with what God's Word directs you to do—because you're just not sure you can trust Him? What steps can you take to bolster your trust in your Mighty God?

DECEMBER 28

WHAT ARE YOU WAITING FOR?

He holds his priesthood permanently, because he continues forever.

{ HEBREWS 7:24 }

JESUS HAS ALL WISDOM. He is our "Wonderful Counselor." Jesus has all power. We are to call on Him as our "Mighty God."

This combination of having all wisdom and all power should be enough to make our faith in Him complete and unquestioned. Being *smarter* than everyone, being *stronger* than everything—what more could we want in this One that we're trusting to help us?

But in Isaiah 9:6 we find yet another reassuring name for Jesus: He is also "Everlasting." Not only can we trust Him then to guide us, not only can we trust Him to strengthen us; we can also "trust in him at all times" (Ps. 62:8) because He will *always* be there to care for us.

Christ has always been. He lived long before His human conception miraculously took place inside Mary's womb. He never began to be. But He also will never cease to be. Jesus Christ "is the same yesterday and today and forever" (Heb. 13:8). He is eternal in His Person. He is eternal in each of His attributes. And, praise God, He is also eternal in His ministry to us as believers. He is both the "author and finisher of our faith" (Heb. 12:2 NKJV). Time is not a factor to Him. "He who began a good work in you will bring it to completion" (Phil. 1:6)—and He is not in a hurry; He has all the time in the world.

Back in Genesis 14, Abraham was met by a mysterious "king of Salem," who, Scripture reveals, was also a "priest of God Most High" (v. 18). This Melchizedek, as the Bible names him, both a priest and a king, extended a blessing to Abraham and received offerings from him in return.

Centuries later the writer of Hebrews devoted a whole chapter to equating Jesus with this visitor from ancient times. Melchizedek appeared to Abraham, the man God had blessed and chosen as the fountainhead of His people. And now we, who by God's grace are blessed to dwell in that stream, continue to receive ministry from Someone "in the likeness of Melchizedek," a king who became our priest "by the power of an indestructible life" (Heb. 7:15–16). Jesus is our "priest forever" (v. 17), one who "holds his priesthood permanently, because he continues forever" (v. 24). His mission of ministering to us continues forever.

We, then, ought to be utterly free from the impatient pressures of worry and ambition, from any doubt in His ability, and from feeling as though the clock is winding down or the window closing on His opportunity to act.

"He has said, 'I will never leave you nor forsake you.' So we can confidently say,

'The Lord is my helper;
I will not fear;
what can man do to me?'" (Heb. 13:5–6)

Today, tomorrow, and till time is no more.

{ *Prayer* }

Forgive my impatience, Lord. I confess I'm too often driven by the crush of time and the setting of deadlines. Free me from such constraints on Your work and from the sense of panic that compels me to demand that You go faster. Let me rest in the ocean of Your eternity. May the arms of my faith stretch all the way out, knowing Your timeline is as wide as it is wise.

{ Keep Reading }

GENESIS 14:17–24

"I have lifted my hand to the LORD, God Most High." (v. 22)

PSALM 110:2–4

"From the womb of the morning,
the dew of your youth will be yours." (v. 3)

HEBREWS 7:26–28

"A Son who has been made perfect forever." (v. 28)

{ Consider }

Our Lord will be here tomorrow, too, you know . . .
and the day after that, and the day after that.
How does the everlasting nature of His ministry
speak to you concerning a specific need
in your life today?

DECEMBER 29

FATHER AND SON

As a father shows compassion to his children,
so the LORD shows compassion to those who fear him.
For he knows our frame;
he remembers that we are dust.

{ PSALM 103:13–14 }

THE TRINITY, AS WE'VE SEEN—the enormity, complexity, and amazing union of this three-in-one God—is a mind-blowing reality. As people who have trouble figuring out how to fold a fitted sheet, we really have no chance of grasping exactly how the Godhead works.

So when Isaiah foretells the coming of Christ—this child to be born, this son to be given—and refers to one of His names as "Everlasting Father" (Isa. 9:6), what are we supposed to make of that?

I say we breathe a humble sigh of acceptance at our limited human comprehension and breathe a deep sigh of relief that our God desires to cover us so completely.

The Father and the Son do have distinct roles within the Trinity, which Scripture reveals to us. And yet there's a sense in which Jesus is like a father to us—the Father of eternity, the Father of our faith. He also fathers us in a personal sense. The Mighty God who fights for us as a champion warrior also rules with the compassion, kindness, and tenderness of a father caring for His children. He is supreme in the universe, but also sweet to our childlike hearts. And, oh, how we need that . . . because it's easy, much too easy, to feel orphaned in this world.

If that's how your heart feels at times, whether literally or relationally, I know those painful emotions can easily be stirred up during the Christmas season. Though you soldier through and keep smiling and serving, sometimes you still ache for someone to care for your soul, someone who isn't there anymore or who doesn't appear to be coming.

I want to assure you today on the basis of God's Word—however hard it may be for you to believe—that the Lord Jesus cares for you, is concerned about you, loves you, and is committed to what is best for you. He is attentive to those who revere Him and trust Him. If you turn to Him, He will father you.

Another great text from Charles Spurgeon—there are so many!—speaks eloquently of Jesus as Everlasting Father: "If you have entered into this relationship so as to be in union with Christ . . . you are His child, and you shall forever be. There is no unfathering Christ, and there is no unchilding us."[11]

Just as a true father never ceases to be caring, kind, and compassionate toward his children, Jesus never ceases to be loving and supportive of you in all the ways you may need a father to do. He is doing it even now, and He will be doing it throughout all eternity. The Son has come and given us Christmas. But He has also come as a Father to give us Christmas blessings all throughout the year.

{ *Prayer* }

Dear heavenly Father, thank You for
Your everlasting love. Thank You for understanding
my need for such all-encompassing care and
for meeting me at every relational level.
Use me, Lord, as one of Your instruments for
ministering to others in my family and community
who need Your tender touch as well.

{ *Keep Reading* }

PSALM 68:4–6

"Father of the fatherless." (v. 5)

ISAIAH 63:7–9

"In all their affliction he was afflicted." (v. 9)

JOHN 10:11–15

"I know my own and my own know me." (v. 14)

{ *Consider* }

How does knowing of the fatherly heart, attentiveness, and compassion of Christ encourage you in your journey?
Who might He want to reach out to and love through you today?

DECEMBER 30

PEACE IN OUR TIME

In his days may the righteous flourish,
and peace abound, till the moon be no more!

{ PSALM 72:7 }

EACH GENERATION THINKS OF ITSELF as being further away from experiencing peace than any other before it. Animosity, bloodshed, conflict, and natural disaster unsettle us and make us anxious, fearful—anything but peaceful.

That wonderful messianic prophecy we've been considering in Isaiah 9:6 says we're being shepherded by the Prince of Peace—*Sar Shalom*, as the Hebrew renders it, "governor of peace." "Of his government and of peace" Isaiah goes on to reassure us, "there will be no end" (Isa. 9:7). Yet as we scroll through the morning's headlines, seeing nothing but armed standoffs and domestic struggles, legal wrangling and political counterpunching, we're left to wonder how this daily snapshot of reality can possibly be squared with an endless reign of peace. The year started out this way, the year kept rolling this way, the next year seems destined for even more of this way.

It's true, at many levels, that we will never experience peace on earth until Christ is ultimately enthroned as King. The Hebrew term *shalom* looks ahead to His visible rule, when "the kingdoms of this world have become the kingdoms of our Lord and of His Christ, and He shall reign forever and ever!" (Rev. 11:15 NKJV).

But peace—*shalom*—is still available to us in the meantime. Because of Jesus' coming, His incarnation, His peace is continually streaming throughout the earth. It runs as an undercurrent of His faithful blessing, flying beneath the cable news radar of world events.

Shalom speaks to a sense of personal well-being, of having our sin-sick hearts and souls restored to health and our relationship with holy God restored. Though terrors may haunt our public spaces and economic instabilities threaten our future security, nothing can destroy the "covenant of peace" (Isa. 54:10) that exists, through Christ, between the Lord and His beloved people.

The word *shalom* also carries the idea of peace between ourselves and others, the restoration of relationships between individuals. The relational complexities of our lives and times, with all the tangling of memories still sore to the touch, can leave us broken and at odds with one another. Each side has a story; each side has a point; the differences can feel insurmountable. And yet inside the free, graceful release of forgiveness—"forgiving each other; as the Lord has forgiven you"

(Col. 3:13)—peace can still bubble up from underneath the hard-frozen ground of bitterness and deal with whatever has separated friends into enemies.

The majority of those in the first century who were watching for any Messiah at all were looking for someone to usher in an era of peace through military might, through the overturning of an oppressive government. But Jesus' mission and government were intended first for human souls, not Palestinian soil. That's why His government has never ceded power, even during days when peace seemed in short supply.

Even in times like these.

{ Prayer }

Lord, thank You for bringing us peace
in troubled times. Thank You for bringing us
the Prince of Peace at Christmastime so we
could continually be reminded of Your willingness,
intention, and ability to establish peace in
our hearts. Raise up pockets of peace, I pray,
throughout our world and throughout
Your Church, for the glory of Your name.

{ Keep Reading }

PSALM 85:10–13

"The LORD will give what is good." (v. 12)

ISAIAH 54:9–10

"My covenant of peace shall not be removed." (v. 10)

2 PETER 3:11–14

"Be diligent to be found by him . . . at peace." (v. 14)

{ Consider }

In what aspects of your life are you experiencing a lack of peace? How might recognizing the undercurrent of God's *shalom* in the world help you move toward peace in your heart? What practical steps could you take to live more peacefully even in a conflicted world?

DECEMBER 31

WHAT A BLESSEDNESS

Blessed be the God and Father of our Lord Jesus Christ,
who has blessed us in Christ
with every spiritual blessing in the heavenly places.

{ EPHESIANS 1:3 }

THE LAST WE SEE OF JESUS ON THE EARTH, He is leading His followers a couple of miles out of Jerusalem toward Bethany. And then, "lifting up his hands he blessed them" (Luke 24:50).

Jesus blessed them. The One whose death had broken the curse—the curse that had hung over the head of every living person since Eden—turned to face His redeemed people, and He blessed them. So beautiful. So significant.

Throughout Scripture, blessings were often pronounced on children by their parents or on subordinates by those in positions of authority over them. To bless other people meant to pray for their well-being, to speak hope into their future, to express desire for God's favor on them long after the person speaking the blessing was gone. Even here, in this historical scene from Luke 24, "while he blessed them, he parted from them and was carried up into heaven" (v. 51). From the sound of it, both things were happening in one continuous motion. Jesus left them, blessing them.

And do you know what Jesus is doing today as we speak? He is blessing us "with every spiritual blessing." I picture Him now with extended hands, gazing upon us with His own eyes in the middle of this moment, blessing His people who now live in fellowship with Him because of His cross.

We're His trophies. He's thoroughly invested in us. The mission that began in His mind before the foundation of the world was always intended to lead here—was absolutely *assured* of leading here. He knew He'd be seated there at the right hand of the Father, having claimed His people for Himself by His blood, and be blessing us. Excited at what His work has accomplished. Excited at what His work is *still* accomplishing.

And so we live today with Him blessing us "with every spiritual blessing in the heavenly places." No way is He going to scrimp on us now after doing all that was necessary to shatter the curse from around us. He gives us everything we need for living out the blood-bought results of our faith in abundant measure.

So be sure of this, my dear sister or brother, as you enter the new year: His blessings are coming to you. Stand and wait for them. Expect them. Make your plans as if they'll continue to come—because they will. They do. They are. *He keeps blessing us*.

One day, in fact, not even the ground underneath our feet will bear this awful curse of sin and death any longer. We'll find ourselves with Him in a place where there is "no more curse," only the "throne of God and of the Lamb" (Rev. 22:3 NKJV), with us, His servants, worshiping Him, blessing Him, and experiencing nothing but His blessing forevermore.

{ *Prayer* }

Thank You for the blessing of spending this
entire last month of the year focusing on You,
daily considering who You are, what You've done,
and what You continue to do. I open my hands
today to receive from You everything You know
I need to serve You and make You known.
May my life sing Your praise and be used
to extend Your kingdom.
In Your blessed name. Amen.

{ Keep Reading }

NUMBERS 6:22–27

"The Lord bless you and keep you." (v. 24)

PSALM 103:2–5

"Forget not all his benefits." (v. 2)

EPHESIANS 1:3–10

"The riches of his grace, which he lavished upon us." (vv. 7–8)

{ Consider }

Begin today making plans to extend to others the spiritual blessings that are daily replenished in your life through Christ. How can this coming year be one of sharing the wealth of His goodness?

NOTES

1. Isaac Watts (1674–1748), "Joy to the World! The Lord Is Come," *Baptist Hymnal 2008* (Nashville: LifeWay Worship, 2008), #181.
2. Robert Lowry (1826–1899), "Nothing but the Blood," *Baptist Hymnal 2008*, #223. The title of this devotional also comes from this hymn.
3. Henry Barraclough (1891–1983), "Ivory Palaces," Hymnary.org, https://hymnary.org/text/my_lord_has_garments_so_wondrous_fine.
4. Anonymous (attributed to Martin Luther), "Away in a Manger," *Baptist Hymnal 2008*, #205.
5. This is not a literal translation, but a linguistic approximation. For more information, see Paul Sumner, "The Hebrew Meaning of 'Jesus,'" Hebrew Streams, http://www.hebrew-streams.org/frontstuff/jesus-yeshua.html.
6. Andrew Murray, *Humility* (Bible Study Tools, 2019), chap. 1, https://www.biblestudytools.com/classics/murray-humility/humility-the-glory-of-the-creature.html.
7. Murray, *Humility*, chap.2, https://www.biblestudytools.com/classics/murray-humility/humility-the-secret-of-redemption.html.

8. C. H. Spurgeon, "His Name—Wonderful," Sermon No. 214, delivered Sunday, September 19, 1858, at the Music Hall, Royal Surrey Gardens, UK, Spurgeon Gems, https://www.spurgeongems.org/vols4-6/chs214.pdf.

9. James B. Irwin, *More Than Earthlings: An Astronaut's Thoughts for Christ-Centered Living* (Nashville: Baptist Sunday School Board, 1983).

10. John Newton, "How Sweet the Name of Jesus Sounds," *Trinity Hymnal* (Suwanee, GA: Great Commission Publications, 1990), #647.

11. C. H. Spurgeon, "His Name—The Everlasting Father," Sermon No. 724, delivered Sunday, December 9, 1866, at the Metropolitan Tabernacle, Newington, UK, Spurgeon Gems, https://www.spurgeongems.org/vols10-12/chs724.pdf.

HEARTFELT THANKS TO . . .

Lawrence Kimbrough – for your skillful, humble collaboration in adapting my teaching into books that inspire readers to "consider Jesus." You are a true servant of the Lord.

Anne Buchanan – for your editorial assistance on this and numerous other writing projects. Your grasp of stylistic and biblical issues, your careful attention to detail, and your wordsmithing ability have made each book better.

My friends at Moody Publishers – for more than twenty-five years of sweet partnership in producing books for His glory and the good and the joy of His people. Eternity will reveal all the fruit.

Erik Wolgemuth, my agent – for your kind support and your relentless care for the many thankless but vital specifics of the writing and publishing process. The Lord sees and He will reward.

Robert Wolgemuth, my DH (Dear Husband) for just over ten years – Your love was a rare and exquisite gift. You earnestly prayed and cheered me through the birthing process of this and each project I undertook during those years. The cavernous hole left in my heart since you went to Heaven will never be filled by anything or anyone less than Jesus. We treasured Him together throughout our marriage. Now your faith has become sight and I long for the Day when I, too, will behold Him in all of His beauty.

Revive Our Hearts
Calling Women to Freedom,
Fullness, and Fruitfulness in Christ
Daily Teaching | Events | Digital Media
Resources | Broadcast Media
For additional teaching from Nancy DeMoss Wolgemuth visit
ReviveOurHearts.com
Your Trustworthy Source for Biblical Truth